In the
the Bene

What Everyone Should Know About Islam

What Everyone Should Know About Islam

IBRAHIM AMINI

TRANSLATED BY
SAYYID HUSSEIN ALAMDAR

Published by the Islamic Seminary Inc.

The Islamic Seminary Inc., New York
© 2013 by The Islamic Seminary Inc.
All Rights Reserved
First Edition 2013
Printed in the United States of America

ISBN: 978-0-9890016-9-4

Alhoda International, Cultural,
Artistic & Publishing Institution

DEDICATION

"In the Name of Allah, the Beneficent, the Merciful"

This book is dedicated to our beloved Holy Prophet Muhammad son of Abdullah (SAW), Seal of the Prophets, his holy progeny — Ahl al-Bayt (AS) — and all devoted scholars and intellectuals who endeavor in the path of grandeur and dignity of Islam; Islamic universal awakening, brotherhood, solidarity and to present the peaceful divine message of monotheism, peace, harmony, coexistence, equality, freedom, justice, love, and human dignity to rescue the mankind through enlightenment at this critical juncture of our contemporary world in the twenty-first century.

Contents

1. Preface

Does this world have a Creator and God or has it been created by itself without any cause? If there is a God then what are His attributes and works? Does God assign an obligation for us, or are we not without some form of responsibility? Were the messengers truthful in their claims or not? Is it possible that after this world there exists another world whereby a human being would see punishment for his/her deeds? The human faculty of reason, in accordance with his primitive nature and special creation, desires to find out about these realities, remove curtains from these mysteries; provide correct answers for these inquiries and many more alike. The human faculty of reason possesses this distinction in it whereby it can distinguish between truth and falsehood and naturally is inclined to discover the realities and causes of things, and until it rests upon an absolute certainty, it does not feel comfortable.

These sorts of topics are called principles of religion *('usul-e-din)*. The principles of religion are topics which are relevant to the thought and soul of human beings, reason and intellect follow it, and deeds and movement of human beings spring forth from its fountainhead accordingly. In the principles of religion *('usul-e-din)* imitation or following is not allowed and everyone is obliged to discover them through his reason and intellect. If a human being, for his beliefs, succeeds in creating a stable and firm groundwork, his intellect and soul feel at ease; he rescues it from internal anxiety, bewilderment, and wandering, and in that case he could continue his life with his conscience at ease and in comfort.

1.1. Childhood and Youth

The best time for nourishment is the period of childhood and adolescence. The fresh page of a mind of a child and a youth is like a photographic film that has not yet been exposed to the light of illumination and is therefore ready for acceptance of any picture upon it. These simple minds, if they could be nourished in a correct manner and if correct thoughts and beliefs could be presented to them with reason and logic, would make a dent upon their sensitive soul and thus would become a permanent temperament of their essence. Such individuals, no matter what environment they are encountered with and whomever they socialized with, would not become deviated and lost. If they happened to be in an impious environment, they would not accept the color of that community; instead they would try to change it to their own color. Unfortunately, this large group has been deprived of correct religious nourishment, and has not yet been paid attention to the way they deserve. Normally they have acquired the religious beliefs from their parents without reason, logic, and program. It is due to this very reason that their faith and belief has not been laid down upon a solid foundation and they do not possess a stable groundwork.

Secondly: They have assumed some of the matters which are baseless and futile as definite religious realities, believed in them, and with the same illogical and initial beliefs and thoughts, enter in primary schools, higher secondary schools and from there into the university environment where they associate with the people of different belief and thoughts. Since the basis of their faith is not firm, or with a slight doubt and criticism, they become easily confused and perplexed, and from the point of knowledge and wisdom have not reached to the extent that they could distinguish truth from falsehood and could separate good from bad. Therefore due to this reason they become cynical with respect to the real religion and remain in the state of bewilderment not knowing what their obligation is supposed to be. Then in that case either they turn their face completely away from religion or at least the basis of their moral ethics or deeds start trembling, causing them to act reckless with respect to their religion. The result of this negligence and incorrect nourishment could be seen explicitly by all and there is no one who could think of a solution in rescuing these innocent individuals from the valley of deviation.

1.2. Everyone is Responsible

Against this greatest danger that threatens the forthcoming generations into irreligiousness and weakness of belief, all individuals of the community are responsible. Guardians of religion, clergies, fathers, mothers, teachers and scholars, speakers, writers and wealthy people, all are responsible. Yes, we are all responsible and if we do not discharge our obligation in this regard, the future generation would send curses upon us and we would be held accountable on the Day of Judgment. We must draw a comprehensive plan and perfect program of implanting correct beliefs with reason and logic inside the brains of the simple minded; and must wage a campaign of confrontation against deviated and wrong beliefs. Educational books with simple language should be prepared for them; libraries must be established for this task; books freely or inexpensive should be provided to them and they should be motivated to read these books.

1.3. The Present Book

The present book has been especially written for the young generation and youths to teach them religious education and the following points have been considered in this book:

1. The contexts while being simple are based upon reason and rationale. Regarding intellectual matters rational reasons have been presented; topics regarding obedience and religion have been presented in accordance with narrations and verses of the Holy Qur'an; if required the source of reference has been mentioned in footnotes, but for the sake of brevity in some topics the sources have not been mentioned.

2. Regarding the date of births and demises of the Holy Prophet (SAW) and Infallible Imams (AS) there are differences of opinion but for the sake of concision one of the quotations has been selected and others have not been mentioned.

3. The writer has tried his best to make the intellectual matters relatively simple so they could be comprehended by all; efforts have been made to avoid usage of philosophical terminology and description of lengthy and tiring arguments.

4. Doubtful, weak and tempered, and less useful matters have not been mentioned.

5. In this book matters have been written whose knowing is compulsory upon every Muslim and whereby the Religion of Islam has been described in a summarized manner in order to prepare the minds of readers to refer to more comprehensive books and journals of the religious authorities *(ris'alah 'Amaliyah* written by *mar'aji').* Especially regarding branches of the religion *(furu'e-din)* all of them have not been mentioned or have been mentioned in summary. The context of the book could be classified into the following three categories:

First: The beliefs *(Aqa'yid)* i.e. matters and affairs which are related to the intellect and faculty of reason a human being, rational reasons rule over them and imitation is not allowed.

Second: Moral ethics *('Akhl'aq)*, i.e. the matters which are relevant to the human self and sentiments, controlling desires of the self, making one's self moderate and placing one's self upon the straight path of humanity.

Third: Branches of the Religion *(Fru'-e-din)*: i.e. mandatory obligations and practical instructions, which are relevant to the human body and what should be done.

In the end I request the readers and intellectuals that if they have opinions or find faults in the book, they should inform the writer so that it could be utilized in the next edition.

Ibrahim Amini
Qum, Islamic Seminary
www.Ibrahimamini.ir

Chapter 1: Theology

1.1. Acquiring of Knowledge

Islam is a religion of education and knowledge; it requires of Muslims that they should seriously endeavor in acquiring knowledge. Islam considers the worth of individuals in accordance with their education and knowledge; it considers acquiring of education as a general obligation upon all Muslims. Allah has said in the Holy Qur'an: *"Are those who know equal with those who know not?"*[1] And say that: *"Allah will exalt those who believe among you, and those who have knowledge, to high ranks."*[2] The Holy Prophet (SAW)[3] has said that: *"Acquiring education and knowledge is compulsory upon every Muslim man and woman."*[4] And he also said: *"The most intelligent person is the one who could utilize from other's knowledge and information and thus increase his own knowledge. The most worthy people are those whose deeds are more and the most unworthy person is the one who is more illiterate than others."* The Commander of the Faithful Imam Ali (AS)[5] said: *"No treasure is more superior than knowledge."*[6]

Imam al-Sadiq (AS) said: *"I do not like seeing your youths except in one of these two conditions: 'Either they should be scholars or*

---

[1]. —*The Holy Qur'an (39:9)*
[2]. —*The Holy Qur'an (58:11)*
[3]. Abbreviation of Arabic, see glossary
[4]. *Biha'r al-Anw'ar*, v.1, p-177
[5]. Abbreviation of Arabic, see glossary
[6]. *Ibid*, p-164

3

students. If it is not so they are negligent, if they are negligent their life would be wasted, whoever wastes his life is a sinner and would enter hell.'"[1] Imam al-Baqir (AS) said: *"Whoever is busy in acquiring knowledge is under the blessing of Allah."*[2] The Holy Prophet (SAW) said to Abudharr: *"Sitting for one hour in a meeting of education and knowledge is superior in nearness to Allah than one thousand nights of prayer that in each night one thousand units of prayer is offered."*[3]

1.2. Theology

This world has a God Who has created it and manages it:

None of the phenomenon occurs by itself without a reason. For example if we see a newly built structure we are certain that it has an engineer, mason and laborers and it has been created due to their efforts and endeavors; we never assume that it has been created by itself without any reason. If we placed a white paper and pen upon our writing table, went outside of the room, and upon returning found that the paper has writing on it, we are certain that during our absence someone came to the table and wrote on it. If a person says that the pen has moved by itself and has written those lines, we

---

[1]. *Bih'ar al-Anw'ar*, v. 1, p-170
[2]. *Ibid*, p-174
[3]. *Ibid*, p-203

would laugh upon his words and consider his statement as illogical.

If we see a painting that contains beautiful illustrations, and attractive scenes that make the viewer fascinated with it, we would say to our own self that: "A skilled artist through his intelligence, art, and powerful hand has turned this worthless page into a precious and valuable work." We are busy talking with a group of our friends in an automobile which was moving speedily towards its destination, suddenly its engine ceases working causing the vehicle to stop; the driver is certain that the engine has not stopped by itself and the stopping of the automobile is not without a reason. None of the passengers inside the automobile have a slight contradiction about it. Because of this reason the driver steps down from automobile and looks at the engine to find out the cause of its stoppage and how to fix the problem, and never says: "Very well, let us wait for an hour or so, perhaps the engine would be fixed by itself and would start working." If your wristwatch stops working, you do not have any doubt that its being stopped is not without a reason, as the movement of its needles was not without a reason, therefore its not working is also not without a reason. Overall you know that no phenomenon is created without reason and a creator and the curiosity of finding its cause is a natural tendency of all human beings.

Now I ask you a question: do you believe in the possibility that this vast world does not have a

God or Creator and could have been born by itself? No, such a thing is never possible. This vast world, this land, large oceans, these stars and great suns, all these wonderful animals, all these beautiful and colorful trees and mountains, and ultimately this large world of existence could not be without a Creator and God.

1.2.1. Order and Discipline of World

If we see a building that has been built carefully with extreme accuracy possessing a complete coordination and arrangement between its various components; for its commissioning everything has already been considered, it does not have any fault and defects, it has water and electricity, a dining room, drawing rooms and bedrooms and its bathrooms are equipped with appropriate ventilation systems and heaters. Piping has been done with extreme accuracy, and water taps and sinks have been provided at appropriate locations. The principles of hygiene have been considered and the sunlight has been used to its maximum advantage; our faculty of reason orders that this well-planned structure has not been created by itself; instead it has a competent and skilled builder who has executed its construction accurately in accordance to the blueprint prepared by the architect and engineer.

After the description of this example, we would like to draw your attention toward a portion of our own daily lives; in order to survive and for the continuation of life a human being requires food and water in order to quench his thirst and satisfy his hunger and to provide necessary requirements for his body cells. So that the mechanism of our body cells remain alive, thus to continue our lives; they must be provided different sorts of food to have plenty of ingredients at their disposal, and their shortage or loss of each one of them would cause problems to our soundness. A human being is in need of air and through this means he absorbs useful portion of air and exhales poisonous gases from the body. Right now let us pay attention to how all these requirements and necessities of our bodies exist outside. If we want food it exists outside, if we want different sort of foods they exist outside, if for our life we need wheat, rice and vegetables, all of them exist outside.

If we want air and water they are present; we have feet in order to go to arrange food, have eyes in order to find out suitable foods, have hands in order to pick up food. Our hands have been created in a manner that it could easily be used to provide all our requirements; they are completely at our disposal, we could move them in every direction, wherever we want, they open and close at will and can go up and down. The precise accuracy and delicacy of our fingers and surface of the hands are truly amazing. We pick up food from our hands and place it in our mouths, our mouth has been designed in a manner that it opens and closes in accordance to our intention. Lips have been created in a manner that they could close to prevent a morsel of food from falling back out.

The basic problem is that even though all of the bodily necessities and various kinds of food exist, it is not so that with their apparent shape they could be utilized by the body's cells; instead changes, work, and precise physical reactions should be performed on the food in order to enable it to be used. The digestion system of the body digests food in four stages and here we would summarize them as follows:

First Stage: Through the means of teeth we chew morsels of food and make them smaller; the teeth which are given to us possess complete coordination with the type of food; the tongue moves inside the mouth and places morsels under the teeth in order to make them very soft. In addition to that like a proactive worker of Customs, it checks and controls of the food, distinguishes good from bad and fresh from the spoiled; salivation glands excrete special fluids so that morsel could become very soft and could be eaten easily; in addition to that, the saliva of the mouth helps to digest food and provides significant chemical effects.

Second Stage: When a morsel is chewed well it enters from the mouth inside the throat and from an unseen path enters inside the stomach; while the morsel goes down, the nasal path is closed and a special curtain closes the respiratory tract or windpipe so that the morsel does not enter inside the respiratory tract.

Third Stage: Food must stay inside the stomach for a time in order to be digested. There exist thousands of minor glands in the stomach wall that excrete special juices and through its means food is digested and turned into something like a flowing fluid.

Fourth Stage: Food enters into the small intestine; the gall bladder and a large gland called the pancreas excrete a special juice upon food which is necessary for its digestion. Thousands of glands exist inside the walls of the intestine and their juices are useful for the digestion of food. In the small intestine the food turns into a diluted form. Then food material is absorbed through wall of the intestine and enters into the blood that carries it to the entire body. The heart through its steady beat pumps blood into the entire body and in this manner each live cell of the body receives suitable food for its proper functioning.

Right now think a little and see; because of the coordination and precise order that exists within bodily parts and other phenomenon of the outside world, is it possible that someone would say that the human being and other phenomenon of the world have been created accidently? If we pay serious attention and pay profound analysis toward the structure of our existence, and look at minor details that have been utilized in the creation of our bodily parts, and order and discipline that exist between our bodily parts and other phenomenon of world, this matter would automatically become clear for us that human beings and other entities have not been created automatically by themselves. Instead they have a Creator Whose precise knowledge and accurate actions has created human beings and has predicted all of his requirements in advance. What power other than the infinite power of a wise and intelligent Creator could create such an amazing order and discipline between phenomena of the world? Has senseless nature created human hands with such proportion and delicacy? Has nature created salivary glands that always keep the mouth moist? Have the guarding curtains over the windpipe, with that serious assignment which they are assigned, been created by themselves? Do not all glands of excretion in the wall of stomach have an intelligent and wise Creator? What power orders the gallbladder and pancreas to discharge the required fluid upon food? Do these two crucial members know about the worthiness of their own existence? What powerful force orders the heart without any pause, day and night to keep it busy in performance of its duty and that it should continue to provide lively material to the vast country of the human body?! Yes, without a wise and Almighty Creator, no one else could maintain such a precise discipline in the phenomena of the world and to manage the magnificent institution of creation.

1.2.2. The Period of Childhood

Right now let us look at another period of our life. When we came to the world we were of weak existence, we could not move in order to prepare food for ourselves, our hands were not powerful enough to prepare food for us, we did not have teeth to chew food, and our stomach did not have power to digest the food. In the period of childhood there was no food suitable for us except milk. When we came to the world the refreshing milk was made available in the breasts of our mothers. Love, liking and affection were placed in the hearts of our mothers in order to love us and guard us day and night and for our nursing, they tolerated all sorts of sorrows and discomforts. After we were grown a little and our hands, feet, eyes, ears, stomachs and intestines acquired relatively more capacity and required to eat heavier foods, little by little teeth started growing in our mouths in order to enable the eating of other foods.

1.2.3. Let Us Make a Judgment

Who has made so much love for us and at the time of our childhood and weakness has predicted all of our requirements? Who has created this vast world of existence, all these large stars, and radiant sun? Who has organized the movement of the moon and earth with such an accurate and precise order? Whose powerful intention has created this orderly rotation of day and night, spring and summer, and fall and winter? Who has created our eyes, ears, tongues, stomachs, hearts, kidneys, livers, intestines, lungs, hands, feet, brains, nerves and other bodily parts with such delicacy and precision?! Is nature, without senses and intention, the cause of the creation of such amazing bodies and bodily parts of human beings and animals, while in the creation of every part like the eye, so much precision and minute complexities have been utilized that specialists, in spite of their extreme and plentiful research are still helpless to dominate all the boundaries and miniature details of that particular part? No, such an act is never possible; rather this is the Most Compassionate God who has created everything and manages this great world of existence.

He is the One Who had always been and exists and bestows existence upon others. God loves his servants and has created all bounties for them. We love the Most Compassionate God and are submissive with respect to Him and obey His commandments, and except Him we do not consider anyone else worthy of obedience and worship, and do not lower our heads in front of those other than Him.

1.2.4. Every Possible Existence Requires a Cause

If we investigate and analyze every existence of the world of creation, think about how its existence has been created; this would be realized by our conscience that it has not been created by itself and its existence is not exactly like its essence. In its state of essence it was without existence and didn't exist. Such an existence is called possible, e.g. if we consider water we would realize this matter conscientiously that water is a reality other than its existence and non-existence. Neither its existence is related with its expediency to exist or not to exist; instead with respect to each of them is un-expedient, i.e. either it may accept its existence or it may accept its non-existence. All incidents of phenomena of the world like water in the state of essence are empty of existence and non-existence. Here your faculty of reason would say: The existences and phenomena of the world in the state of their essence do not exist, if they want to exist, another external element or factor should remove this defect of their personal essence and bestow upon them existence. The existence at the state of their essence is needy and destitute until and unless someone else should not remove their poverty through the bestowment of the dress of existence upon them, they would not be present.

All world phenomena which lacks essence and possess the potential of their existence, do not possess any independence and existence from themselves, terminates into a perfect, needless, and an independent existence, whose existence should exactly be like His essence and non-existence and annihilation should not exist for Him. Such perfect existence is known as a being or thing, Whose existence is necessary *(W'ajibul Wujud)* or God of the Worlds. God's essence is exactly His existence;

non-existence and annihilation could not be imagined for Him. He is permanent with His essence and other creations are needy of and dependent upon Him and acquire existence through His existence.

1.3. God's Characteristics

Overall God's characteristics could be classified into two parts:

1.3.1. Provable Characteristics

Every characteristic which exists from real-perfection, increases worth of its object, making its essence more perfect without the condition of not requiring a body and being susceptible to change for the object which is being characterized is called a provable and elegant characteristic like: Knowledge, power, life, speaking, and intention. If we compare two existences with each other that one of them is a scholar and the other one is illiterate, we could realize it with our conscience that the existence of the scholar is more perfect, effective, and worthy than the illiterate. Therefore on this basis it could be said that knowledge is one of the characteristics of a real existence. Other characteristics of perfection can be identified on the basis of the same comparison. The God of the Worlds possesses all characteristics of perfection and elegance and all of them are permanent for His essence. In order to prove this matter two reasons could be sufficient:

First Reason

Every perfection, goodness and prosperity that exists in the world all has been created by God and He has bestowed worthiness upon existences. Because the created beings for their real existence are needy of God, in the perfection of their existence as well in their beauty they are needy of Him. Since the real existence has been bestowed upon them by God and they do not possess any independence by themselves, perfection of existence too is received by them through God. Thus, the Creator of existences and their characteristics of perfection is God.

Now if you take a brief pause, your faculty of reason would say: God who has bestowed all these perfections to His creations could not have His own essence without these perfections. If He does not have them, it was not possible to bestow those things upon others. Because, the fountainhead and origin of perfection cannot be assumed of not having them in it; a lamp until it is not illuminated cannot provide illumination to others. Oil if it does not contain fat cannot make others things fatty. If water itself is not wet, it cannot make other things wet.

Persian Poetry

"Zat na'ya'fteh az hasti bakhsh,
Kay tawa'nad ke shaved hasti baksh."

15

Translation

"Essence not obtained by the One Who bestows existence,
   How could it ever provide existence to others?"

Second Reason

The Essence of God is absolute existence that does not possess any sort of limit and defect, since it is not limited and imperfect it is not needy of others and has not obtained His existence from others; i.e. He is (a being or things) Whose existence is necessary *(W'ajib al-Wajood)*. Therefore, on this basis each characteristic that exists from perfection is permanent for God and His essence with respect to it, does not have any boundary and limit and would not be empty of it. If the essence of God does not have perfection it would be limited and needy and would not be a being or thing Whose existence is absolutely essential and inevitably would not be self-sustaining. Therefore, from this reason and the previous one it could be said that the Essence of the God of Worlds from every dimension is perfect and is infinite and possesses all perfections of existence and provable characteristics.

1.3.2. Some Provable Characteristics

1. Power: God is Almighty and Powerful; i.e. every possible task that He wishes, He could

16

materialize; is not helpless from any task, with respect to each task is not compelled and helpless, For His All-mightiness, there is no limit and boundary and His power is infinite.

2. Knowledge: God is wise and intelligent, i.e. He knows everything and encompasses over all creations and world phenomena and there is nothing hidden from Him.

3. Life: God has life and is alive; i.e. He is a being that does his work in accordance with Knowledge, power, and intentions. God is not like others live beings who are identified through the means of their movement, respiratory system, and eating food, but since He performs acts with knowledge, power, and intention, life is proved for Him.

4. Intention: God does His works through intentions and determinations and is not like fire that does not have any intention in burning; God's existence is a perfect existence that does work with intention and unlike subjects without intention, He is not defective.

5. Seeing: God is a Seer and has sight i.e. sees all visible incidents and phenomena of the world and none of them are absent from his sight.

6. Hearing: God is a Hearer and hears, i.e. He hears all hearable things and is not negligent with respect to any sound.

7-8. Ancient and Eternal: God is ancient, i.e. He always had been, and He was never without existence i.e. non-existence is not possible for Him. He is eternal and would always be, and annihilation and destruction for Him is not possible. God is absolute existence and His existence is exactly like His essence. Due to this reason, He does not need others for His existence; He always had been and would remain forever. No one has bestowed upon Him existence that could be taken away. God is superior to time and timely creations, and does not have a past and future.

9. Speech: God is a Speaker, i.e. He could explain realities for others and could make them to understand His determinations.

These sorts of characteristics are called provable characteristics which are valid for God's essence.

1.3.3. A Necessary Reminder

Since we are imperfect in our essence and characteristics, i.e. are unable to do works without mental intention and bodily parts. We have power but without the interference of our bodily parts are unable to perform any task. We have power of hearing but cannot hear without ears and hearing nerves. We have power of seeing but cannot see without eyes and nerves related to sight. Since God's essence is at an infinite degree of perfection

18

and the same is true to His characteristics, He sees without eyes, hears without ears, works without bodily parts, and understands without brain and nerves.

The path of seeing and hearing is not that it should only be materialized through the means of eyes and ears; in a manner that if seeing and hearing is done without paying attention to it, we say: it is not hearing and seeing. But the reality of seeing and hearing is not except that it should not remain hidden and covered from the seeing and hearing person even if they are materialized without means of his attention. Our essence and academic credentials too, if were not limited and imperfect, we could have seen things without eyes, and without ears could have heard, certainly seeing and hearing would have been valid upon them. Like in the state of our sleeping we could see and hear without natural ears and eyes. Since the God of Worlds from the point of view of essence and characteristics exists at the infinite state of perfection, His deeds and acts too are different from the acts of human beings, and any sorts of need and defect do not have any entry into His works.

1.4. Characteristics of Essence and Deed

God's provable characteristics overall could be classified into the following two categories:

1.4.1. Characteristics of Essence

The characteristics which are always permanent for God's essence and their proofs do not require a pause upon anything else are called characteristics of His essence; like knowledge, power and life; these characteristics always have been permanent and their proof does not depend upon anything else, and instead are exactly like His essence. God was knowledgeable and still is, even before he had created any creatures. He was powerful before His creating anything that was possible for him to create. God always had life. His position of essence is not without knowledge and power otherwise it would be limited, defected, and needy and would not be a being or thing Whose existence is necessary *(W'ajib al-Wajood)*.

1.4.2. Characteristics of Deed

The characteristics that are taken from some of God's acts are called characteristics of acts, like that of the Creator, Provider, Benevolent, and Forgiving. Since He creates the creatures, He is called the Creator, He provides them their sustenance and is called Provider, since He bestows upon His creatures, He is called Benevolent, and since he covers our sins and faults He is called Forgiver of sins. These types of characteristics in reality prove a sort of special communication which exists between God and His creatures.

1.4.3. A Narration

Husain ibn Khalid said: *"I heard from Imam al-Rida (AS) who said: 'God had always been knowledgeable, powerful, alive, ancient, a seer, and listener.'* I said: 'O son of the Holy Prophet (SAW) a group says: 'God had been knowledgeable but had more knowledge than His essence, had been Almighty but had more might than His essence, had been alive but with more life than His essence, had always been ancient but older than His essence, had been a listener but more hearing than His essence, had been a seer but could see more than His essence.' Imam al-Rida (AS) replied: 'Whoever considers God's characteristics additional to His essence is a polytheist and would not be considered as my follower. God had always been knowledgeable, Almighty, alive, ancient, a listener, and a seer but these characteristics are exactly like his essence.'"*[1]

1.5. Attributes that cannot apply to God

Characteristics that cannot apply to God are called the attributes that cannot apply to God. God's essence is perfect and does not have any defect and fault; any attribute that could be considered a defect for God is not applicable to Him.

---

[1]. *Bih'ar al-Anw'ar*, v. 4, p-62.

1.5.1. Some Attributes that cannot apply to God

1. God is not compounded

Everything which is created by two or more components is described as being compounded but God is not compounded and does not have any other part, because every compound requires another thing; without that thing it is impossible to be created. If God too is compounded, inevitably He would require another thing, and an essence that is needy and defected could not be (a being or thing) Whose existence is necessary *(W'ajib al-Wajood)*. In addition to that every compound requires a cause that could organize the components and with their mixing it could be materialized. If God too is compounded, He too inevitably is needy of a cause and an essence that is defective and needy could not be a being or thing whose existence is necessary.

2. God is not a Body

God is not a body because a body is a compound and earlier it has been proven that God is not compounded, therefore He would not have a body. In addition everybody needs a place and space in order to be created in it and would not have its existence without a place. While God is the creator of places and is not needy of them. An existence which has a body and requires a place could not be a being or thing whose existence is necessary.

3. God is Unseen

That is He cannot be seen through the means of eyes, because only bodies and properties possess the ability to be seen by eyes, while it has been earlier proved that God is not a body. Therefore He could not be seen.

4. God is not an Illiterate and Ignorant

Because in the discussion of negative attributes it was proved that God is knowledgeable about everything and there exists no limit or boundary for His knowledge. Therefore ignorance and illiteracy are faults and defects that do not have an entry into God's perfect existence.

5. God is not Helpless and Powerless

Because earlier in the discussion of power it was proved that God is Almighty and Powerful to perform any task and is not helpless from the performance of any task; for His infinite power no limit or boundary could be imagined. Being helpless and powerless is a great defect that does not have any entry in God's perfect existence.

6. God's Essence is not a Place of Incidents to Occur

Change and transformation do not have entrance into His existence; He does not get old, and sick; does not forget and make mistakes, does not have to sleep and experience fatigue; He does not feel ashamed in performance of an act because these sorts of attributes are the effects of the material and body and since earlier it was proven that God is not a body or matter, therefore it is not a place for occurrence of such incidents.

7. God does not have a Partner

The reason of this matter would be given in the discussion of Monotheism.

8. God does not have a Place

God does not have a place and is not located in space, neither in heaven nor in earth, because He is not a body to be confined in a place.

God is the creator of places; therefore He is higher and superior than places and does not have any need for them. Since He encompasses all of the existences, none of them are able to part take in His existence; He is everywhere and encompasses all existences; but not in the sense of a great body that has occupied all material worlds from one end to another; instead He is an absolute existence and is not limited into any limit or boundary; He is not committed to any place and space; He has complete domination over all existences and is not separated from them; here and there is not applicable to Him.

The fact that at the time of prayer, we raise our hands towards heaven is not that we consider God in the heavens rather we want to express with these means our degradation and helplessness and desires to manifest the state of sorrow of a destitute. If we name the mosque and the Holy Ka'ba as the House of God, it is due to the reason that God is worshipped there and He himself has bestowed nobility to these places.

9. God is not needy

He does not need anything or anyone; because God's essence is complete from all dimensions; He does not have any defects so that he would need help from others. If he needs a thing He would be limited and defective and would not be something whose existence is necessary.

And if He has assigned obligations and duties it is not in the sense that He is in need of our prayers, fasting and other worships, instead through the means of worship and performance of good deeds, our self and soul become perfect and illuminated, in order to acquire worthiness to utilize eternal bounties of paradise for our life in the hereafter.

And if He requires that we should pay charity *(zakat)* one-fifth yearly savings *(khums)*, alms *(sadaqah)*, do favors toward our fellow human beings, and should act as a vanguard in charitable affairs, it is not in the sense that He is in need of our material help. But since paying charity and one-fifth yearly saving, recommended alms, and attention toward charitable affairs are required for managing the social affairs of society and are in the interest of the general community, He has made their payment mandatory. Regarding alms and the foundation of charitable trusts for benefits of the general public He has made plenty of recommendations. In addition, munificence of wealth in the path of God, and taking care and helping the distressed, foundation of charitable trusts, in themselves are great acts of worship that become a cause of one's self perfection and achieving the rewards hereafter.

10. God is not a Tyrant and Oppressor

This argument would be dealt with in the discussion in the chapter of justice.

1.6. Monotheism

God is one and does not have any partner in creation. God is Almighty of the world of existence and without Him there is no creator who could bestow existence. God has created all existences small and large and in their creation does not require help of anyone because of a several reasons:

First Reason

Had there been two gods, it would not have been outside of the domain of the following factors:

First Probability

That each one of those two gods, as an independent would have created all existences; i.e. each existence would acquire its existence twice and each god would create it directly. With a little pause, the falsehood of this assumption would be proven; because each existence does not have more than one existence and from this consideration cannot have more than one creator. After God had bestowed upon him an existence, it is not possible that another cause too bestows upon him another existence.

Second Probability

Two gods with cooperation and help of each other created creatures in a manner that every creature is created by two gods, and each one of the gods is a part of the cause and half of the doer. This probability too is baseless and void, because if cooperation of these two gods is due to their defect and need, each one of them alone, without help from the other would be helpless and incompetent to create anything, then such defect and incompetency are not compatible with their being god. And if it is said: each of them alone could create the world but at the same time they cooperate with each other and with the cooperation of each other create existences like some people in lifting a piece of heavy stone cooperate while each one them alone too could lift that heavy stone. This probability too is not correct; because two causes and subjects that could undertake the task alone, if they disregard their independence and seek help from the power of each other and with cooperation and help perform that task, it is not without reason.

Either they want to utilize less energy or want to remain immune from opposition and hindrance of the other. Either they are scared, panic with each other or in summary require help and cooperation of each other. While the need and destitution of any sort does not have an entry about God. In addition to that since each one these two supposed gods possess knowledge and have power about creation of the world, and his knowledge and power is exactly like his essence, miserliness does not have any entry into His existence, He must be a single and independent cause in creation of the world and in accordance with his knowledge and power should manage it. That would mean that both of these supposed gods alone and with independence could create the world while it has been proved earlier that the effect of two independent causes in a single consequence is impossible.

Third Probability

The two supposed gods divide world existences between them and each one of them with independence creates a group of existences and interferes in existences created by the other god. Such a probability is also false, because each one of these two supposed gods with respect to existences which happen to be the share of the other god, possess power and knowledge of reformation. Therefore he should also be the creator and god of them, which requires that two causes must affect a single consequence whose falseness has already been proved. If he does not or is incompetent in creation or is a miser, again he is defective and does not possess the worthiness of being a God.

Second Reason

If one these two supposed gods creates an existence and another one decides to destroy it, if the first god is able to defend his creatures and could prevent the work of another god, the second one is helpless and would not be a god. And if he could not defend his creatures, he is helpless and therefore would not be a god.

Result of Monotheism

Since we believe in the unity of God, and consider Him as Lord of the worlds, other than Him, whoever and whatever it may be, we consider as weak and incompetent. Except God-Almighty we do not consider anyone else owner and worthy of worship and obedience; we do not fall upon the dirt in front of anyone else. For other than God we do not express servant-hood; we do not give away our freedom and intention under the control of anyone. In front of another human being, we do not perform infinite respect and praise; we consider his appeasement and flattering as a defect. With regards to Messengers, Imams, and religious leaders we respect them and obey their instructions due to the reason that God has made their obedience as mandatory. Their decrees and instructions always have been under the radius of divine commandments and never transgress from these limits.

We go for the pilgrimages of Messengers and Imams and pay respect toward their tombs, but not with the intention of worshipping a deity, rather with the intention of respect and honor for their spiritual status, infallibility and holiness. We construct their holy tombs, inhabit them, go for their pilgrimages; in order to pay our tributes for their exalted distinguished position and their religious sacrifices, and in order to make others comprehend that whoever suffered in the path of God and endeavored for the admonishment and guidance of the people would not be forgotten even in this world. In the holy tomb of those pious and selected individuals of God which are a sacred place, offer silent prayers, ask our needs and forgiveness from God, Almighty through the means of placing the sacred souls of those pious individuals as our intercessors.

1.7. Justice

God is just, does not oppresses anyone; a disgusting and shameful act is not done by Him; all of His acts are in accordance with wisdom and expediency; He does not keep the deeds of pious ones without rewards, He never breaks His promise, never tells a lie, and does not take innocents to hell for two reasons:

First Reason

Whoever oppresses, or performs a shameful deed is not out of three possibilities: either he does not understand the evil of that shameful act and because of this reason commits that oppression. Or he is aware about the ugliness of his oppression, but sees things in the hand of others that he himself does not have and is in need of that, oppresses them so that he himself could utilize the belongings of others that were obtained by them through performance of hard work. The owner who oppresses his workers and wastes their wages, or tyrants who transgress upon the rights of feeble and destitute; indulges in that oppression that he considers himself from the point of view of wealth and power as deficient, and therefore through means of usurpation of other's belongings and wealth, which were obtained by them through hard work, fulfills his own needs. Or he is aware about the evil of his oppression, does not need but for the sake of taking revenge or seeking pleasure engages in oppression. Every oppressor inevitably possesses one of these motivations but the God of the Worlds does not oppress; because ignorance and unawareness cannot be imagined for Him since He is knowledgeable about all interests, dimensions, good and evil of the act. He is absolutely needless and does not need anything and any act. Nonsense and vain acts are not done by Him; therefore injustice about Him cannot be imagined.

Second Reason

The faculty of our reason understands that oppression and tyranny is an undesirable and evil act; all faculties of reasons are unanimous about this matter. God too through the means of appointed messengers has commanded people not to perform tyranny and oppression. Therefore, on this basis how it's possible that God would perform an act that is considered as an evil by all intellectuals and God himself has prohibited it? Of course all human beings are not similar and are not located at the same level; instead from the point of view of poverty and affluence, beauty and ugliness, intelligence and ignorance, soundness and defects differences are observed between them. Some of the individuals are encountered with severe hardships.

Unpleasant tragedies and hard diseases are encountered by some individuals, but all of them are consequence of a series of natural causes which are inseparable requirements of the material world and material things and in the creation of the material world there is no escape from them. Natural causes and occasionally sometimes human beings themselves have interference in their existence. However from God there are no prohibitions from acquiring blessings and every existence in accordance with his personal talents and in harmony with natural causes and circumstances is enabled to acquire blessings from God. He never forces anyone to perform an act beyond his capacity and power. Endeavors and hardships of individuals would never be wasted, and for every individual to the extent conditions and circumstances assist, the path of advancement and progress remains open.

Chapter 2: Prophethood

2.1. Prophethood

It is incumbent upon God that for the admonishment and guidance of human beings, He should appoint messengers and necessary commandments and laws should be provided to them.

Reason of this Matter

The purpose of creation of the human being is not only limited so that he should live in the world, utilize divine bounties and with thousands of efforts and endeavors, tolerance of different sorts of hardships; that he should complete the short and limited portion of his age and then die and disintegrate. If it is so then the creation of human beings and the world would be nonsense and void and the sacred threshold of God, the Wise, is glorified from undertaking nonsense and void acts.[1] Instead the human being has been created with the intention of being higher and the most exalted one in the creation of existence. God has created human beings in order to learn distinctions and perfections of humanity in order to acquire the decency and worthiness that he should be able to achieve ranks, positions, and rewards in the hereafter.

Therefore a human being is needy for a complete program, commandments, and laws that one side should organize his worldly life and should

---

[1]. *Did you think that We had created you for a playful purpose and that you were not to return to Us?"*
—The Holy Qur'an (23:115)

prevent from transgressions and threats upon him through assuring his freedom, comfort, and rights. While on the other side should provide him the path of human perfection, straight path, honesty, and return to God and should teach his perfections and distinctions of his self, make him aware of evil conducts and deviated factors; but the short and limited faculty of reason of a human being is unable to create such complete commandments and provide to a nation because firstly: Knowledge and information of human beings is limited and incomplete, it does not have sufficient information regarding different sort of needs of human beings, dimensions of good and evil, and how to encounter with limitations and laws. To prove the correctness of this statement that human being from birth until, now has endeavored to create complete laws for the management of the society, plenty of hardships have been done in this path and a significant amount of budget has been spent but until now has not been able to obtain desired laws. Every day he passes a law but it does not take very long that he discovers its defects, and therefore either decides overall to void it or through ratification of a note tries to reform it.

Secondly: The motivation of self-interest and egotism of human legislatures never permits them to close their eyes from their own interest as well as the interest of their associates and to look at all human beings with the same scale, or to consider the interests and benefits of a general people. And whenever they decide to disregard their self-interests and prejudice and do it for the sake of pretending, eventually this stubborn nature dominates upon them and whether intentionally or unintentionally forces them to follow the path of their own selfish interests.

Thirdly: human legislatures are ignorant of spiritual perfections and virtues and do not have any information regarding spiritual life; they do not consider the prosperity of human beings except through the dimensions of material means; while the worldly life of a human being is not separate from his spiritual life and a very profound relation exists between them.

It is only the Creator of men and worlds Who encompasses all dimensions of good and bad for the human being and knows well the path of perfection and prohibition from dangers. He is able to provide commandments and laws which assure the prosperity of world as well as of the hereafter for a human being. It is because of this reason that we could say: A wise God never releases a human being in the valley of distress and ignorance; instead his infinite benevolence requires that through means of his appointed messengers from the race of human beings, to provide them required commandments and a program. The messengers are distinguished appointed persons who are in a position to establish communications with the God of worlds and could receive realities; and could declare to the people accordingly, such type of communication is called a revelation that is unique and a special communication which is established between His messengers and God. A messenger through the means of esoteric eyes witnesses the realities of the world of existence, with his heart's ears hears words from the unseen and announces them to the people accordingly.

2.2. Conditions of Prophethood

1. Infallibility

The prophet must be infallible i.e. should have unseen power that should allow him not to commit sins and should remain immune from mistakes so that God's commandments that have been sent for guidance of the people without more or less should be provided to them. If the prophet himself commits sins and should act in opposition to his own words, his words would lose the essential credit and worthiness. If through his own deeds he makes his own words null and void and practically leads people towards sin and opposition of God's commandments and this matter cannot be contradicted, that propagation with deeds is more effective than the propagation of words. If the prophet happens to be negligent and makes mistakes, he would not be trusted and his words would become worthless.

2. Knowledge

The prophet should be knowledgeable about all commandments and laws, which are necessary for the prosperity of the world and hereafter of human beings. And he should not be ignorant about any topic which is necessary for the guidance and admonishment in order to be able to present them the real path of perfection and programs for the prosperity of human beings in a complete form; and could introduce the straight path of human prosperity — that is not more than one and among its components there exist very profound communications.

3. Miracles

The miracle is an outstanding act, which occurs through means of other than natural causes, and human powers are helpless in the creation of such an act. Since a prophet claims that which is opposite to the natural trend, he is able to communicate with the unseen worlds and the God of the worlds and could obtain knowledge and learning; and claims that he has an assignment from God to perform the task of guidance of the people, he should introduce commandments and laws of God, he must do something to prove his claim. That should not be the normal tasks of human beings and their power should be helpless in producing a similar act, so that through this means he could prove his task of prophethood and communication with the God of worlds that in itself is an abnormal act; such an act is called a miracle. In summary since a prophet claims communication with God, therefore he must show types of Godly acts, in order

41

to prove his claim that he has the power of communicating with God.

However, let it not remain unsaid that programs of prophets were not that they should have completely taken off their hands from the natural causes and resources and should have only resorted to miracles for every task; rather wherever they thought it was expedient to prove their prophethood through performance of a miraculous act, in such cases they did perform miracles.

2.2.1. Path of Identification of a Prophet

It was proved that a messenger or prophet possesses an outstanding position and rank that he could communicate with God and through means of revelation could receive realities; the prophet possesses extraordinary, special infallibility and is immune from sins and mistakes, and it is obvious that identification of this important mysterious position is not the task of everyone. It was due to this reason through the means of one of these two paths one could identify the prophet and could conclude his being as truthful:

First Path

That another prophet had already proved his Prophethood, through his testifying or should predict about his arrival in advance and should describe his indications and effects.

Second Path

That in order to prove his truthfulness of his word he should be able to bring a miracle that human beings should be helpless in creating of its like. When human beings saw that a person claims prophethood and says that he is appointed by God for your guidance; in order to prove the truthfulness of his words he performs an act that could not be performed through a human being, seeing that act they attain certainty of his being truthful. If he was a liar, God would not have supported him through the means of a miracle, since the testifying of a liar is relevant to ignorance and indecency and God does not indulge in indecent acts. Therefore in order to diagnose the position of infallibility and prophethood another path does not exist except these two paths.

However let it not remain unsaid: For intellectuals and researchers another path remains open, they could study commandments and laws and investigate them profoundly and then should compare these laws with laws and could appreciate their distinctions and benefits. In the conduct of words and deeds of a person claiming prophethood they should show serious and precise curiosity and through these means of witnessing and testifying should acquire the facts about his being truthful. But perusing of such a path is not possible for every one and except for testifying the position of prophethood and strengthening the power of belief; it does not have any worth. In the Holy Qur'an regarding a group from prophets, miracles have been mentioned: Whoever considers the Holy Qur'an as a heavenly book, inevitably must accept about the story of Prophet Moses' (AS) staff turning into a serpent, and the dead coming back to life and the return of sight to a blind person since birth through the means of Jesus (AS); the story of speaking in the cradle by Jesus (AS) is certainly a part of the Holy Qur'an.

2.2.2. Number of Prophets

It has been mentioned in the narration that 124,000 have been sent by God for the guidance of human beings, the first one of them was Adam (AS) and the last one of them was Muhammad ibn Abdullah (SAW).[1] The prophets could be divided into several categories as follows:

Some of them received their duties through the means of revelation but were not assigned the responsibility of propagation. Another group was assigned the responsibility of propagation; some of them possessed special religious laws and religion while others didn't bring special religious laws instead propagated the religious laws of another prophet and very often many prophets were busy in undertaking their duties in various regions and cities. Noah (AS), Abraham (AS), Moses (AS), Jesus (AS), and Muhammad (SAW) were distinguished prophets and brought special religious

---

[1]. *Biha'r al-Anw'ar*, v. 11, p-30.

laws and were called as men of decision *(ulul-azm)* prophets. A group of prophets have the book, like Noah (AS), Abraham (AS), Moses (AS), Jesus (AS) and Muhammad (SAW). Some of them were appointed for the entire humanity while some of them were appointed for a particular group of people.[1]

2.3. Muhammad (SAW) - Seal of the Prophets

Muhammad son of Abdullah (SAW) was one of the great and most distinguished among them and is a prophet of Muslims. When he was appointed for his prophethood, due to the continuous and prolonged hardships and the painful endeavors of past prophets, the religious learning level of human being reached to the point whereby they were in a position to receive the best and most perfected laws and could comprehend the highest leanings; they should guard forever the trust of knowledge of all prophets, then the Prophet of Islam was appointed and he presented the most complete program and comprehensive commandments for the human beings.

If the commandments of Islam been implemented, the prosperity of the world and hereafter would have been assured as they were sufficient for guidance of humanity during the period of the Holy Prophet (SAW); likewise they

---

[1]. *Ibid*, pp, 1-61.

are sufficient for the prosperity of the present period as well as for more progressive forthcoming generations. Everyone who would conduct research with accuracy and precision regarding Islamic commandments and learning and would compare them with other commandments; the distinction of Islamic commandments would become explicitly clear upon him. And it was because of this reason that he is the last prophet and after him no prophet would come. The matter of being the Seal of the Prophets for Muhammad (SAW) is a necessary requirement and whoever denies it would not be considered as a Muslim.

2.4. Eternal Miracle

The Prophet of Islam possessed miracles that occurred during his life period and they have been pointed out in the books of history and narrations; in addition to that the Holy Qur'an is an eternal miracle and absolute certification of his prophethood. The Holy Qur'an itself introduces it as a miracle and declares officially to the people: *"And if you are in doubt concerning that which We reveal unto Our servant (Muhammad), then produce a surah of the like thereof, and call your witnesses beside Allah if ye are truthful."*[1] And says: *"Say: Verily, though mankind and Jinn should assemble to produce the like of this Qur'an, they couldn't produce the like thereof*

---

[1]. *—The Holy Qur'an (2:23)*

46

though they were helpers one of another. "[1] Although the enemies of Islam didn't stop from taking any sort of action in their confrontation against Islam and readied them for the dangerous and bloody wars, and in this path suffered plenty of financial and physical losses, but in spite of that were unable to confront with the Holy Qur'an of Muhammad (SAW) and could not produce a similar verse. While if such an act was possible, for them they certainly would have preferred it to difficult confrontations in order to rescue them from all those headaches and hardships.

The blessed Holy Qur'an was descended gradually during a period of twenty-three years upon prophet Muhammad (SAW). His companions wrote exact revelation called signs *(a'ayat)* that were collected later on and was then presented as it is in the current form. The Holy Qur'an is the only heavenly unique book in which any sort of changes or deviations have not been made, and without more or less is available for mankind; the Holy Qur'an is a book of deeds. If the Muslims desire to be prosperous and could raise their heads in dignity, to acquire back their lost majesty and grandeur; they do not have any other option except to follow the steady and firm program of the Holy Qur'an, and its implementation should cure their untreatable pains and social problems.

---

[1] *—The Holy Qur'an (17:88)*

2.5. A Brief History of Holy Prophet's (SAW) Life

His father's name was Abdullah and his mother's name was A'aminah. He was born on the seventh day of Month of Rabi al-Awwal in the year called the Year of Elephant *(A'am al-Feel)* in the Holy City of Mecca; he was appointed to prophethood at the age of forty years. He remained in Mecca for thirteen years and during this period he invited people towards Islam openly and secretly, during this period a group of people believed in him but the pagans and idol-worshippers with their complete stubbornness interfered and prevented the advancement and progress of the Islam. They made serious efforts and endeavors in torturing Muslims and the Holy Prophet (SAW) to the extent that his own life was threatened with danger, then he was forced to migrate to the Holy City of Medina; gradually little by little the Muslims too joined him there and eventually the Holy City of Medina was turned into the prime capital of the Islamic Government and its military garrison. The Holy Prophet (SAW) continued propagation of commandments, guidance of the people and administering social affairs for a period of ten years; the Islamic Army continuously remained at the alert position for defense and war.

The Holy Prophet (SAW) lived in this world for a period of sixty three years; he passed away on the twenty-eighth of the Month of Safar in the eleventh year of migration, and was buried in the

Holy City of Medina. Since his childhood, he was well mannered, truthful and righteous and due to this reason he was called as Muhammad, the trusted one *(amin)*; from the point of view of good moral ethics he was the most famous among the people of his period. Treachery and lying were never noticed with respect to him, he never oppressed any one, never performed indecent acts, treated the people with respect, was well mannered and courteous, showed favor and compassion towards the destitute and distressed; whatever he said, he acted upon it accordingly and it was due to the means of his loveable manners that people were inclined towards Islam and became Muslims with their own determination.

Imam al-Sadiq (AS) said: *"A beggar came near the Holy Prophet (SAW) and asked for help, he got a little amount of dates from a helper as a debt and gave it to him; a little time passed but the means of paying the debt were not available to him. One day the person to whom he was indebted came and demanded his dates, he replied: 'Right now I do not have them, whenever I am in a position to do so I would return them to you.' He came again and heard the same reply from him. At the third time when he arrived and heard the same reply, he said: 'O Prophet of Allah! Until when will you keep saying, God-willing, I would pay?' The Holy Prophet (SAW) while encountering his impolite reply smiled and said: 'Is there anyone who would give me dates as a debt?' A person replied: 'O Prophet of Allah, I would give you.' He*

49

said: 'Pay this man such amount of dates, the creditor said: 'I do not demand more than half of this quantity; the Holy Prophet (SAW) replied: 'I have bestowed the remaining half quantity upon you.''' [1]

2.6. Islamic Laws

The Islamic laws are not only limited to worshipping, commandment and individual obligations, rather it consists of a comprehensive social order and has commands and a program in various arenas of human beings; it has laws and programs regarding social, political, legal, and civil affairs. The Holy Prophet (SAW) and the Commander of the Faithful Imam Ali ibn Abu Talib (AS) governed the Muslims through the execution of the same laws; Muslims in the beginning of Islam through means implementation of the same programs were able to achieve all those advancements and astonishing progress, and established a powerful and magnificent government. We believe that the laws of Islam are better and more perfect than all the laws; if they could be executed completely between mankind and if they could be utilized for administering society, mankind would attain prosperity and goodness, oppression and tyranny would be completely rooted out, piece and coexistence would replace wars and confrontation; and poverty and unemployment would be totally eliminated.

---

[1]. *Haya't al-Qulub*, v.2, p-168.

We believe that: The laws of Islam are not defective and do not require reformation and completion. We know that the sacred Islamic ideology understands real interests of the people and has provided them the very best laws. We believe that every law that is against the Holy Qur'an is not in the interests of the people and does not have any worth. We believe that we should follow the Islamic commandments and the Holy Qur'an in all areas of life in order to become prosperous. We know that the horrible state of affairs of Islamic nations has not been created because of the effect of Islam; instead their entire affliction is because of their refusal of the implementation of Islamic laws. Since, we left the Islamic laws behind and required medicines of sickness for our social problems from others, and only sufficed ourselves in the name of Islam, we have fallen into such a dark day.

We believe that if Muslims want to regain their lost prestige, dignity and grandeur and join the lines of progressive and advanced nations, they have no options except to become the real Muslims, and should implement all commandments of the Holy Qur'an and should take inspiration from its social programs. But so far the laws and programs of Islam remain only written with ink upon paper, and have not been implemented in their totality; we should not wait for progress and grandeur.

Chapter 3: Imamate (Leadership with Divine Authority)

3.1. Imamate (leadership with Divine Authority)

In the discussion of prophethood, it was proven that it was essential that God, the Wise, should dispatch messengers for the guidance of mankind, should provide them with the laws and commandments so that they could achieve prosperity and perfection; now we say that: Since the life of messenger is not eternal in the world and through his demise it is quite possible that divine commandments which came for the guidance of mankind might have been destroyed. Therefore, after the prophet there must be someone so that divine commandments without any less or more addition should remain preserved near him; he should make efforts and endeavor in guarding and preservation of those commandments; he should guard the religion and execute the divine commandments, which guarantee the prosperity of mankind. He should look after for the worldly and religious deeds of the people, so that the path of achieving the prosperity and perfection for the human beings remains open and the link between God and the people should not be disconnected; such a person is called an Imam or successor.

The Imam is a protector of the treasure of knowledge of the Prophet; the Imam is the most perfect manifestation of a human being as well as of religion. He is leader of the people; he himself takes a spiritual journey of perfection and prosperity as well as guides others.

3.2. Characteristics of an Imam

1. Infallibility

The Imam too, like a prophet, should be immune from making any mistake or negligence in remembering commandments, their propagation, and execution so that the divine commandments should remain with him without any less or more; and he should not allow the people to deviate from the straight path of honesty in execution of commandments and administration of the society; the main road of perfection–which is not more than one–should not be obstructed. The Imam should be infallible and immune from the performance of any sin and rebellion. And his deeds should be in compliment with his words, so that his words and values should not lose credit and should not lose his confidence and trust from the people. If he would commit sins, deeds opposite to the religious commandments, he would become as an example for the people and through means of his character would invite them to oppose religious commandments. Thus, the Imam must be infallible i.e. he should act upon all religious commandments and should be decorated with the esoteric essence of the religious commandments.

2. Knowledge of Imam

An Imam must know all divine commandments of the religion. He must be thoroughly knowledgeable with respect to every aspect relevant to his spiritual position and leadership. He should be a learned scholar *(a 'lim)* to possess all religious commandments with him, so that in guidance and administration of the people, he should not be helpless and incompetent; he should be able to keep the straight path of prosperity open.

3. Distinctions and Perfection

Earlier it was proven that an Imam acts upon all religious commandments and undertakes his journey in the context of religion. Therefore, he should be the most superior and most perfect human being. He journeys upon the straight path of religion and accompanies others with him and guides them. An Imam is a total manifestation of the religion, and in his blessed existence all realities and divine learning could be witnessed.

4. Miracles

It could be utilized from history and narrations that the infallible Imams (AS) like Prophets had miracles and were capable of performing acts which were not possible by ordinary human beings. Occasionally the circumstances required that proof of their position of infallibility and imamate depended upon their performance of a miracle. Whoever would refer to the books of narrations, their excellent virtues, history, and with unprejudiced intellect should review the abundance of miracles that have been attributed to the Infallible Imams (AS) and would attain the certainty that overall they had possessed miracles and outstanding works. Of course it is not our intent that all miracles that have been related to the Infallible Imams (AS) are true and correct; instead perhaps among them some false and unknown matters might have been existed.

5. Imam's Identification

An Imam could be identified through two paths:

First Path

The Prophet or the previous Imam should introduce him and appoint him as his successor and leader of the people. If he is not introduced by God, Prophet and previous Imam, the people by themselves could not identify the Imam, and could appoint him as their leader for their governmental affairs; because it was proven earlier that an Imam and leader of the people should be infallible, most distinguished and learned scholar of the community. Other than God no one else has knowledge about the position of his infallibility. Ordinary people are not in a position to diagnose the infallible from the non-infallible. Regarding perfection of his holy essence and divine knowledge no one knows except God and Prophet.

Second Path

In order to prove his Imamate, if an Imam has performed an outstanding act or miracle, his imamate would be proven because had his claim been a lie, God would not have certified his credibility through the means of a miracle.

Difference between an Imam and Prophet

Imam and Prophet have differences between them from the following point of views:

First

A Prophet is the founder of a religion and is a bringer of the religious commandments while an Imam is the guardian of commandments and is responsible for their execution.

Second

A Prophet receives the religious laws and commandments through the means of revelation and has direct communication with God; but an Imam is not a receiver, i.e. the laws and commandments are not revealed upon him instead he receives them from the Prophet and has a vital role in the guidance, and admonishment of prophetic knowledge.

3.3. Appointment of a Successor and Number of Imams (AS)

Whoever in the society possesses a position and rank and is responsible for its ruling affairs, if he wants temporarily not to go to work, without any doubt, he appoints a successor for himself and assigns responsibility of ruling affairs of the society upon him. He would never be ready to leave that congregation or community without assigning a supervisor or manager. The Holy Prophet (SAW) of Islam too paid a serious attention about this task and assigned plenty of emphasis regarding this matter. Every village or city that was conquered at the hands of Muslims, he immediately appointed a ruler and governor for it. When he dispatched soldiers to the war-front, he assigned a commander for them and also he occasionally assigned his replacement in case of his martyrdom or sickness. Whenever he journeyed or participated in a war, he appointed his successor and assigned the ruling affairs of the community in Medina to him.

The Holy Prophet (SAW) was the ruler of the Muslims, he was not negligent about this matter that after his demise the Muslim society requires an infallible ruler, who through means of execution of divine laws and commandments should administer them and should make efforts and endeavors towards the advancement of his cherished objective. The Holy Prophet (SAW) knew well that Islamic nation could not remain as a living, powerful, and Islamic nation without an infallible ruler. Due to this reason it could be said with absolute certainty that: The Holy Prophet (SAW) with all that compassion that that he had for overall discipline and order of the Islamic community and survival of Islam; it was impossible that he would leave the world without appointing a successor or leader for ruling affairs of the young Islamic nation. Apart from that it was proven earlier that an Imam should be appointed through God and Prophet because except God and His Prophet, no one else could testify to his infallibility.

Therefore it is absolute duty of the Prophet to introduce an infallible Imam to the people and if he has acted negligently in this regards, he has left the matter of prophethood and propagation of religion as incomplete. It is because of this reason that we are certain that the Holy Prophet (SAW) has declared his successor and Imam of the Muslims. The Holy Prophet (SAW) not only appointed the successor immediately after him, instead he also introduced the forthcoming Imams after him. In plenty of traditions that have reached to us through the Holy Prophet (SAW) the numbers of the Imams have been declared as twelve. The Holy Prophet (SAW) said: *"There would come twelve caliphs after me and all of them would belong to Qureshite. The first person of them would be Ali (AS) and last one would be the promised Mahdi (AS). And in some of narrations the names of all twelve persons have been mentioned."*[1]

---

[1]. Refer to *Ghayat al-Mura'm*, *Ithbat al-Huda*, *Yanabi' al-Mawaddah*, *Sahhih Abu Da'wood*, and *Musnad-e Ahmad.*

3.4. First Imam (AS)

The Holy Prophet (SAW) from the beginning of his appointment until his death has introduced at several occasions Imam Ali ibn Abu Talib (AS) as his successor and an Imam. In the last year of his life he was blessed of performance Hajj-pilgrimage in Mecca. While, he was returning from the journey, and reached at a place called: *Ghadir-e-Khum,* a verse was revealed upon him: *"O Messenger! Make known that which hath been revealed unto thee from thy Lord, for if thou do it not, thou will not have conveyed His message. Allah will protect thee from mankind. Lo! Allah guides not the disbelieving folk."*[1]

The Holy Prophet (SAW) stopped his journey right there and ordered that all Muslims should stop their journey. More than twenty thousand people gathered around him; he ordered that a pulpit should be made; he went upon the pulpit and took Ali ibn Abu Talib (AS) in his hands and raised him so that the people could see him. He delivered a sermon and said: *"Upon whomsoever I am the master and guardian, Ali too is his master and guardian, O Allah whoever likes Ali, Thou should be his friend and whoever does enmity with him You too should do enmity with him."* Omar was the first person who made allegiance with Ali and said: *"O Ali! Congratulations you have become my master and guardian as well as of*

---

[1]. *—The Holy Qur'an (5:67)*

other believers. " After Omar, other Muslims too made allegiance with Imam Ali (AS). It was in this manner that under extreme heat and burning sun of Hejaz, that important task was materialized, and Imam Ali (AS) was officially appointed to caliphate and Imamate.[1] This important incident was held on the nineteenth of Dhu al-Hijjah in the tenth year of migration, and in order to remember this historical day, we Shi'a celebrate that day as a feast called: *Eid-e-Ghadir.*

Imam Ali (AS) was born on thirteenth of the Holy Month of Raj'ab, in Mecca twenty three years before the migration; his father's name was Abu Talib and his mother's name was Fatimah. Since his childhood, he was placed under the direct care of the Holy Prophet (SAW) and was the prime individual who believed in him. The Holy Prophet (SAW) married his daughter Fatimah al-Zahra (SA) and thus he became his son in law. His distinctions and services are so vast that it is impossible to describe them. He was matchless and unique in bravery and manhood; participated in wars and was always in the forefront and never feared any one waged war in support of Islam, and motivation of God's worship; while encountering severe hardships and dangerous incidents, never spared

---

[1]. *Al-Bidayah wa al-Nihayah,* v. 5, p-208; a group of Holy Prophet's (SAW) companions have narrated the story of *Ghadir-e-Khum,* this narration is continuous and certain and exists in the Shi'a and Sunni books. The relevant narration in the book of *Ghayateh al-Mur'am,* has been mentioned eighty nine ways from Sunnis and forty three times from Shi'a.

himself from showing self-sacrifice and risking his life. He was unique in worshipping and piety; was matchless in wisdom and knowledge and was the treasure of the Holy Prophet's (SAW) knowledge. So far it was possible, he confronted with oppression and injustices and defended the oppressed, showed compassion and kindness towards destitute and helpless ones. Imam Ali (AS) loved agriculture and engaged himself in tree plantation, habitation of uncultivated lands, and construction of aqueducts.

When the Holy Prophet (SAW) left this world a group of hypocrites decided to dismiss Imam Ali (AS) from the caliphate. They disregarded and ignored his personal perfections and distinctions and remained naïve with all those recommendations of the Holy Prophet (SAW) and removed Imam Ali (AS) from the caliphate and succession. Taking the excuse that Imam Ali (AS) was young and not suitable for the caliphate; had killed plenty of groups in the wars and due to this reason people had grudges against him, and therefore would not tolerate his caliphate. During the caliphate of Abu Bakr, Omar, and Othman, which went on for twenty-five years, Imam Ali (AS) was forced to sit alone in a corner where he trained and nourished worthy individuals. After the killing of Othman, people took allegiance with him and for approximately four years and nine months he ruled the Muslims. He lived in the world for sixty three years and on the night of nineteenth of Holy Month of Ramadan in the fortieth year of migration, was struck a blow upon his head by Ibn Muljim's hands in the Mosque of Kufa and martyred on the night of twenty first of the same month and was buried in the Holy City of Najaf in Iraq.

A Story from Imam Ali (AS)

The person in charge of the treasury of the Islamic Government said: *"A necklace of pearls was present in the treasury. One day a daughter of the Commander of the Faithful, approached me and borrowed the necklace and said: 'I am celebrating the feast of Eid al-Adha, would return it after three days, and in case it get lost I would pay you its cost.' The Commander of the faithful saw the necklace in the neck of his daughter and recognized it and asked me: 'Why have you committed a treachery regarding general wealth of the community?' I explained him the matter and said: 'Your daughter assured me that it wouldn't be lost, and I myself also guarantee about its return; he said: 'Right now take it from my daughter and if after that you would do so I would punish you'; the daughter said: 'O my dear father! Do not I have that much right to borrow the necklace for three days to celebrate the days of Eid al-Adah?!' Imam Ali (AS) replied: 'O daughter of Ali, do not transgress from your right! Do all immigrant women have such a necklace to decorate themselves with it during the days of Eid al-Adha?'"*[1]

---

[1]. *Man'aqib A'le Muhammad*, Ibn Shahr 'Ashub, v.2, p-108.

Another Story

One day Imam Ali (AS) saw a woman who was carrying a water skin upon her shoulders to her home. He said: *"Give the water skin to me so that I could bring it to your home, in between the path to her house he asked that woman how she had been; she replied: 'Ali ibn Abu Talib dispatched my husband to one of the frontiers of the country where he was killed. A few orphan children have remained from him, and do not have the food and clothing, I am forced to work as a maid to earn a living for them; Imam Ali (AS) carried that water skin to her house and then returned, and spent the night in anxiety and sorrow. In the morning he carried a bag full of food to her home and said to that woman: 'Open the door, I have brought food for the children.' She replied: 'May God be pleased with you and judge between me and Ali.' Imam Ali (AS) entered inside home and said to the mother of the children: 'Do you want to cook the bread and let me take care of the children or vice versa?' The women replied that I am more familiar with cooking of the bread and you take care of the children. Imam Ali (AS) kept the children amused and as well-cooked the meat; when the bread was cooked Imam Ali (AS) with his own blessed hands put the bread and dates into the mouths of the orphaned children and said: 'O the light of my eyes eat and be contended with Ali.' A woman from the neighborhood identified that honorable one and said to the widowed woman that: 'This man is the Commander of the Faithful.' That woman came near Ali (AS) and said: 'O Commander of the Faithful! I am ashamed from you.' Imam Ali (AS) replied: 'I am ashamed from you because until now I was negligent about yours affairs.'"*[1]

3.5. Second Imam (AS)

Imam Ali (AS) because of God's command appointed his son Imam al-Hasan (AS) for Imamate.[2] Imam al-Hasan (AS) was born on the fifteenth of the Holy Month of Ramadan in the Holy City of Medina in the third year of migration. His father was Ali (AS) and mother was Fatimah al-Zahra (SA) −daughter of the Holy Prophet (SAW). The Holy Prophet (SAW) loved al-Hasan (AS) and al-Husain (AS) very much and said about them that: *"al-Hasan and al-Husain are best youths of the Paradise.*[3] After the demise of his exalted father Imam al-Hasan (AS) reached to caliphate and Imamate but was encountered with serious opposition from Mu'awiyah who was the ruler of Syria. Eventually his opposition lead to military confrontation and the armies of Imam al-Hasan (AS) and Mu'awiyah stood against each other; when Imam al-Hasan (AS) reviewed the general affairs of his soldiers, he witnessed treachery from a majority of his commanders. Therefore he avoided

---

[1]. *Bih'ar al-Anw'ar,* v.41, p-52.
[2]. *Ithbat al-Huda,* v. 5, p-373.
[3]. *Yanabi' al-Mawaddah,* p-373.

war and was forced to have a peace with Mu'awiyah. The basic reason of peace of Imam al-Hasan was due to two reasons:

Firstly

Although the number of the soldiers was significant, they were divided and disorganized. Among them there were plenty of individuals who were hypocrites and were supporters of Mu'awiyah; they had even promised to arrest Imam al-Hasan (AS) and hand him over to Mu'awiyah. Imam al-Hasan (AS) realized that if he wage a war with a disorganized and hypocrite army, defeat was absolutely certain; apart from that through the means of severe internal warfare, bloodshed and continuous confrontations, plenty of groups who were supporters were getting killed and the Muslim manpower was weakening.

Secondly

Mu'awiyah with his shrewdness tricked the people and through means of pretending and cheating, presented himself as supporters of the religion and defenders of the oppressed and said: *"I do not have any other objective except advancement of Islam and implementation of commandments of the Holy Qur'an."* But Imam al-Hasan (AS) knew that: *"Mu'awiyah is lying and does not have any other aim except continuation of his rule, but was it possible to make people comprehend this matter easily?!"* It was due to this point and other considerations that Imam al-Hasan (AS) decided for peace in order to expose the filthy personality of Mu'awiyah and his dangerous plots to the people so that the nation could understand very well about Mu'awiyah and the institution of Bani Umayyah so that ultimately the grounds for a revolution could be made readied.

Imam al-Hasan (AS), for the protection of the fundamentals of Islam made peace with Mu'awiyah and in the peace treaty mentioned these conditions, but Mu'awiyah did not respect any one of them. Imam al-Hasan (AS) lived in this world for a period of forty-seven years. Eventually with the encouragement of Mu'awiyah with the hand of his wife Ju'adeh binte Ash'ath, he was poisoned and martyred on twenty-eight day of the Month of Safar, and was buried in the Jannatul Baqi' Cemetery in Medina.

A Story from Imam al-Hasan (AS)

A Syrian man saw Imam al-Hasan (AS) in the path and started calling him with insults. When he ultimately became silent, Imam al-Hasan (AS) paid attention towards him, saluted, smiled and said: *"I assume that you are a stranger in the town, perhaps you have misunderstood the facts, if you offer an apology, I would be contended with you, if you need anything I would provide it to you, if you are a destitute I would make you needless, if you are exiled I would provide shelter for you, if you have any special need, I would bestow upon you; I have plenty of wealth and a large house, if you enter into my home and be my guest, it would be better for you.*" After the Syrian man heard these words, he wept and said: "*I testify that you are the Caliph of God and Imam. God knows better where to place the Caliphate and Imamate. O son of the Holy Prophet (SAW), before our meeting you and your father were the worst enemies near me; but at present I consider you as the most superior creatures of God, then he entered into his house and as long as he lived in Medina, was the guest of that noble one.*"[1]

3.6. Third Imam (AS)

Imam al-Husain (AS) was born on the third of the Holy Month of Sh'aban in forth year AH in Medina, his father[2] was Imam Ali ibn Abu Talib (AS) and his mother was Fatimah al-Zahra (SA), daughter of the Holy Prophet (SAW). Imam al-Hasan (AS) through God's command appointed his brother Imam al-Husain (AS) to Caliphate and Imamate. During Mu'awiyah's Caliphate; he lived under very severe and harsh conditions because the commandments and laws of religion were not executed, and God and the Holy Prophet's (SAW) commandments were replaced with Mu'awiyah's personal whims and desires. Mu'awiyah's institutions did not leave any stone unturned in the destruction of Ahl al-Bayt (AS) and Shi'a of Imam

---

[1]. *Man'aqib A'le Muhammad,* Ibn Shahr 'Ashub, v. 4, p-19.
[2]. *Ithbat al-Huda,* v. 5, p-169.

Ali (AS). With all these unpleasant circumstances, he practiced patience and self-restraint until Mu'awiyah died and his son Yazid became his successor. Yazid ordered the Governor of Medina to seek his allegiance from Imam al-Husain (AS) and in case of his refusal, he should be executed.

The Governor of Medina announced Yazid's orders to that noble one; Imam al-Husain (AS) requested permission of one night in order to think about the situation. But since he did not consider the allegiance and signing of Caliphate in the interest of Islam and his life was in danger, he was forced to move towards Mecca and to stay inside the immune sacred sanctuary of God; thus he moved towards Mecca and entered it on the third of the Holy Month of Sh'aban. The story of Yazid and Imam al-Husain (AS) and his movement was circulated among the cities. The people of Iraq who were opposed to the Government of Mu'awiyah and Yazid, especially the people of Kufa, wrote a significant number of letters to Imam al-Husain (AS) and invited him to Iraq.

On the other hand Imam al-Husain (AS) realized that Mu'awiyah and Yazid had trampled all commandments of the Islam. In order to secure their rule and position they had not hesitated to commit all sorts of illegitimate acts, tyranny and oppression. They ruled in the name of Islam and considered themselves as successors of the Holy Prophet (SAW); there was a fear that they would completely turn fundamentals of Islam as upside down. Now they wanted of him that he should testify the authenticity of their government officially; on the other hand Yazid has secretly assigned a group to murder the Imam al-Husain (AS) in Mecca, or they should arrest him alive.

It was under these circumstances that Imam al-Husain (AS) decided that in order to secure the basic essence of Islam, confront the injustice of Bani Umayyah, and guard the sanctity of the House of God, he should leave Mecca and should rise up against Yazid's tyrannical institution. Thus, he moved towards Kufa which was the center of the Shi'a, they had promised their support and cooperation, and perhaps to achieve his lost rights to confront Bani Umayyah. Yazid's Army besieged and didn't allow him to reach Kufa. Then the order arrived from Yazid that if Imam al-Husain (AS) surrenders take allegiance with him, dispatch him towards me so that I could decide about him, and in case if he did not surrender, fight with him. Imam al-Husain (AS) did not give himself to wretchedness, he did not make compromise with the tyrant Government of Yazid; instead he fought, and with his small army stood up against the huge army of Yazid. He fought with perfect valiancy and bravery and killed a group of his enemies. Ultimately, he himself, his brothers, and sons drank from the chalice of martyrdom; they were killed on the tenth of Muharram in the year 61 AH, and were buried in Karbala, Iraq. Imam al-Husain (AS) lived in this world for a period of fifty-seven years.

We Shi'a consider the Day of 'Ashura as day of sorrow and lamination and for the remembrance of epic and valiant martyrdom, organize large congregational assemblies so that the spirit of self-sacrificing and confrontation against injustice and oppression should remain alive among the nations. The objective of Imam al-Husain (AS) was defense of religion and confrontation with oppression, we too never forget about this sacred objective. Imam al-Husain didn't surrender his body to degradation and wretchedness and taught Muslims to offer self-sacrificing and extreme devotion. Imam al-Husain (AS) was killed but was not defeated. He made the supreme and distinguished virtues of human beings alive forever; practically taught the people self-sacrificing, extreme devotion, righteousness, and confrontation with injustice and tyranny. He was able to expose and degrade Yazid and Bani Umayyah who were ruling in the name of Caliph of the Holy Prophet (SAW), and proved their shameful deeds as false. He made the pillars of Umayyad Governments tremble and destroyed their dangerous plot against the Islam. Organization of assemblies of crying and lamination only in itself does not insure the exalted objective of Imam al-Husain (AS), instead his sacred objective must be identified and efforts and endeavors should be made for its pursuit accordingly.

3.7. Fourth Imam (AS)

The fourth Imam, Imam Ali ibn al-Husain (AS), was born on the fifteenth of Jamada al-Thani 38 AH in the Holy City of Medina. His father was Imam al-Husain (AS) and mother was Shaher Bano, daughter of the Yazdgerd, Emperor of Iran. Imam al-Husain (AS) appointed him for Caliphate and Imamate through God's command.[1] Imam al-Sajjad (AS) made so many efforts and endeavors in prostration and worshipping that he was called al-Sajjad and Zain al-A'abidin. He was present in the incident of Karbala but since he was sick, he was not killed (in battle); during his journey from Karbala to Kufa and Damascus he delivered eloquent speeches and proved the sacred objective and truthfulness of his exalted father and the heart-burning, horrible tragedy of the Martyrs of Karbala and their path of honesty to the attention of the general masses.

Since Imam al-Sajjad (AS) did not have freedom and was not in a position to propagate Islamic learning and knowledge and commandments of religion among the people, he was forced to sit in isolation. He kept himself busied in worshipping God and utilized opportunities to nourish and train the individuals. In order for the publication of religious learning he pursued another path; i.e. he presented religious learning in the form of prayers. Excellent prayers

---

[1]. *Ithbat al-Huda*, v. 5, p-212; *Irsh'ad* of Shaykh Mufid, p-238

have remained from him; one of this most precious works consists of the book of: *Sahifeh Sajjadiyeh*; Imam al-Sajjad (AS) lived in this world for 57 years and on twenty-fifth of the Month of Moharram in the year 95 AH, he was martyred in Medina and was buried in the Baq'i Cemetery. Imam al-Sajjad (AS) liked that orphaned children, blind, crippled, and the destitute should appear at his table-spread and many times he gave them food by his own blessed hands; he provided food and dress for many poor people of Medina. During the night when the people were sleeping he carried the food upon his back and covered his face so that no one could identify him.

He went to the doors of poor and destitute and distributed food among them; it happened very often that the deserving ones were standing upon doors of their house waiting for the arrival of Imam al-Sajjad (AS). When they saw him, they gave the glad tidings of his arrival to each other but no one identified him and knew who the source of their food was. When Imam a-Sajjad (AS) died the poor of Medina understood that unidentified man was Imam Zain al-A'abedin (AS) and it was only then that the sound of their loud cries were raised.[1]

---

[1]. *Man'aqib A'le Muhammad,* Shahr 'Ashub, v. 4, p-153.

3.8. Fifth Imam (AS)

Imam Muhammad al-Baqir (AS) was born on third day of the Month Safar in the year 75 AH in Medina. His father was Imam Ali ibn al-Husain (AS) and his mother was Fatimah, the daughter of Imam al-Hasan Mujataba (AS). Imam al-Sajjad with God's command appointed Imam al-Baqir (AS) to the Caliphate and Imamate.[1] His education and knowledge was so much that he was titled as the one who reaches the depth of knowledge *(Baqir al-Uloom)*. The great scholars recognized his intellectual position and were humbled in front of him and respected him in a manner like that of a school child who sits respectfully before his teacher; they asked their problems from him and received sufficient answers. For Imam al-Baqir (AS) an opportunity arose that was not provided to all of his predecessors. Due to internal conflicts and confrontations of the caliphs, he had relatively more freedom and seriously endeavored in the publication of Islamic learning, religious commandments and laws, and left thousands of educational contexts and narrations as his legacy.

Imam al-Baqir (AS) lived in this world fifty-seven years and was martyred on the seventh day of the Month of Dhu al-Hijja in the year of 114 AH, and was buried in the Baq'i Cemetery. Imam al-Baqir (AS) loved agriculture and worked hard to earn his livelihood. Muhammad ibn Mankader said:

---

[1]. *Ithbat al-Huda*, v.5, p-263; *Irsh'ad* of Shaykh Mufid, p-245.

"On a very hot day I met Imam al-Baqir (AS) in the vicinity of Medina, I saw that he had gone out for agricultural affairs and sweat was dripping from his body. He said to himself that: 'For an honorable and exalted person like Imam al-Baqir (AS) who is an offspring of the Holy Prophet (SAW), it is not decent to come out of his home in this heat, I better admonish him. I went near him and offered salutations upon him, while taking deep breaths and while his sweat was dripping he answered my salutations. I said: 'O Son of the Holy Prophet (SAW)! Is it not insulting that at such a time you are busy in seeking the world? If your death arrives right now what would you do? That honorable one rested his back against some support and said: 'If my death arrives right at this time, I would die in the state of worshipping; because I am working so that I do not stretch my hand from begging near you or other people. If I am in a state of sinning against God, then in that case I must be scared from death.' I said: 'O the Son of the Holy Prophet (SAW), I wanted to admonish you but I become admonished from your words.'"[1]

3.9. Sixth Imam (AS)

Imam Ja'far al-Sadiq (AS) was born on seventeenth day of the Month of Rab'i al-Awwal, in the year 83 AH. His father was Imam Muhammad al-Baqir (AS) and his mother was Umme Farwah,

---

[1]. *Kashf al-Ghummah*, Printed in Tabriz, v. 2, p-337.

the daughter, of Qasim ibn Muhammad ibn Abu Bakr. Imam al-Baqir (AS) with the command of God appointed Imam Ja'far al-Sadiq (AS) for the position of Caliphate and Imamate.[1] During Imam al-Sadiq's (AS) period the confrontation between Banu Umayyah and the Abbasids had intensified significantly and as a result the power of the current government was rather weak. Banu Abbas too, in their opposition with Banu Umayyah, supported Ahl al-Bayt (AS). Imam al-Sadiq (AS), utilized this opportunity and endeavored in education of religious learning and publication of commandments and laws; through organizing educational assemblies, he nourished distinguished pupils and intellectuals; and succeeded in introducing education of issues relevant to legitimate *(halal)* and illegitimate *(har'am)* among the people.

Approximately four thousands[2] pupils were trained in the School of Imam al-Sadiq (AS); books consisting of precious treasurers were written from traditions. Due to this reason the Shi'a School of Thought is called as the Ja'fari School of Thought. Imam al-Sadiq (AS) lived in this world for a period of 65 years and was martyred in the Holy City of Medina in middle of the Month of Raj'ab or twenty-fifth of the Month of Shawwal in the year 148 AH and was buried in the Baq'i Cemetery.

---

[1]. *Ithbat al-Huda*, v.5, p-328; Irsh'ad of Shaykh Mufid, p-254.
[2]. *Irsh'ad* of Shaykh Mufid, p-254.

3.10. Seventh Imam (AS)

The seventh Imam Musa ibn Ja'far al-Kazim (AS) was born on seventh of the Month of Safar in the year 128 AH in Abw'a that has been located in between Mecca and Medina. His father was Imam al-Sadiq (AS) and his mother was Hamideh. Imam al-Sadiq (AS) with the Command of God, appointed his son Musa to Caliphate and Imamate. His worshipping and piety was to the extent that he was called Righteous Servant *(Abd Saleh)*; he was very mature and compassionate and never lost his temper while encountering severe hardships, and due to this reason he was called repressor of anger *(al-Kazim)*. In spite of the fact that the Imam (AS) lived in a very difficult period, there was no opportunity for the publication of narration, even then, plenty of people acquired knowledge from his presence and plenty of narrations have been left from him.

He lived in this world for 55 years; in the year 179 AH, Caliph Harun ordered that he should be taken from Medina to Iraq. He was imprisoned for years in Baghdad and Basra and ultimately was poisoned and martyred on twenty-fifth of the Month of Rajab in the year 183 AH. He was martyred in prison of Sindi ibn Sh'ahak in Bagdad and was buried in the Holy City of Kazmain. A man in Medina continuously bothered Imam al-Kazim (AS) and cursed Imam Ali ibn Abu Talib (AS); some of companions of the Imam (AS) said: *"Please permit us to kill this wicked person, he refused them to do*

79

that and instead asked them where that person was?' They replied: 'He is busy in agriculture in the vicinity of Medina.' Imam (AS) started moving in the direction of his agriculture farm; he reached near him, sat near him, with a smiling and pleasant face asked him: 'How much have you spent on this farming?' He replied one hundred dinars.' He asked: 'How do you expect your return?' He replied: 'Two hundred dinars.' He asked how much do you want to earn from it.' He replied: 'Two hundred dinars.' Then Imam (AS) gave him a sack containing three hundred dinars and said to him: 'The product of this farming also belongs to you.' That man who saw such sort of benevolence against his annoying of Imam (AS), stood from his place and kissed Imam's (AS) forehead and asked pardon from his previous insults; Imam (AS) pardoned him and returned towards Medina. The next day they saw that man in the mosque, and his eyes fell upon Musa ibn Ja'far (AS) he said: 'God knows better where to place His Prophethood and Imamate. The people were amazed and wanted to find out the reason of change in his behavior, that man started talking about the virtues and distinctions of Imam Musa ibn Ja'far. Then Imam Musa ibn Ja'far (AS) said to his companions: 'Was this act better than your decision? Through the means of an insignificant amount of money I have removed his evil and have changed him into a friend of Ahl al-Bayt (AS).'"[1]

---

[1]. *Kashf al-Ghummah*, v.3, p-18.

3.11. Eighth Imam (AS)

Imam al-Rida (AS) was born on the eleventh day of the Month of Dhu al-Q'ada in the year of 148 AH. His name was Ali, his father was Imam Musa ibn Ja'far (AS) and his mother's name was Najmah. With God's Command Imam Musa ibn Ja'far (AS) appointed his son Ali to Caliphate and Imamate.[1] The knowledge and learning of Imam al-Rida (AS) was superior with respect to all of the people of that period. Students for acquiring knowledge came to his threshold and utilized from his presence; a large number of narrations about Islamic learning and religious laws and commandments have remained as his legacy. He had very interesting debates and arguments with the scholars of other religions. He participated in the debate assemblies and answered criticisms of all, and was not helpless in answering about each issue whatsoever.

His vast learning and knowledge made the people present amazed and causing them to offer him praise and compliments; he was regarded among the people extremely honorable, and was called as Scholar of Holy Progeny of the Holy Prophet (SAW). Caliph Mamun al-Rashid in the year of 200 AH called Imam al-Rida (AS) from Medina to Marv, located in the Khorasan Province of Iran. When Imam al-Rida (AS) entered into

---

[1]. *Ithbat al-Huda*, v.6, p-2; *Irsh'ad* of Shaykh Mufid, p-285.

Marv, Mamun suggested that Imam (AS) should accept the Caliphate, but he didn't accept; with a great deal of insistence he suggested that he should accept becoming the successor! He, with this act, had two intentions:

1. He wanted, by appointing Imam al-Rida (AS) as successor, to acquire a religious and spiritual pretense in order to attract the attention of Shi'a and Alawite S'adat towards him and through this means, make him at ease from their opposition and rebellion.

2. He wanted Imam al-Rida (AS) to accept becoming his successor to become close to the Institution of Caliphate and become involved in the affairs of the country and through this means sacrifice his prestige and dignity to lessen Shi'a inclination, attachment toward him.

Imam al-Rida (AS) was well-informed with respect to Mamun's intentions and knew that: Someone, in order to secure his caliphate, does not even hesitate to kill his own brother; it is not possible that with pure intentions, he would offer caliphate or the position of successor to someone else; however due to these illegitimate reasons he refused to accept becoming his successor, but with the intense pressure of Mamun, he had no other option except to accept it. However, he did so with the condition that he would not interfere in affairs of the country and in appointments and terminations of the rulers. Later on Mamun realized that Imam al-Rida (AS) had not given up his honor and dignity, instead, the inclination and attachment of the people with respect to the Imam was increasing day by day. It was due to this reason that he decided to kill him.

Imam al-Rida (AS) lived in this world for 55 years then he was poisoned through Mamun and in the last Month of Safar in year 303 AH, was martyred in Tus and was buried in the same place which is now called the Holy City of Mashhad.

3.12. Ninth Imam (AS)

The ninth Imam (AS) was born on the tenth of the Holy Month of Rajab or on the nineteenth of the month of Ramadan in the year 195 AH in Medina. His name was Imam Muhammad al-Taqi (AS), his father was Imam al-Rida (AS) and his mother was Sabikah. Imam al-Rida (AS) with God's Command appointed Imam Muhammad Taqi (AS) for Caliphate and Imamate. Imam Muhammad al-Taqi (AS) attended the Imamate after his father. Although at that time he was in his childhood and had not attained the age of the puberty, God's given knowledge was so much that that he was able to answer all the religious problems of the people. The difficult religious questions that were asked for his testing were replied to very well; in a manner that his knowledge and distinctions became explicit for the ordinary people and they were all amazed with his power of knowledge.

His piety and piousness was to the extent that he was called as the most virtuous *(al-Taqi)*. Imam al-Jawad (AS) lived in this world only for twenty-five years; the Abbasid Caliph Motasam called him from Medina to Baghdad, in the 220 AH, where he was martyred on the last day of the Month of Dhu al-Q'ad'a in the same year in Bagdad and was buried near the grave of his grandfather Musa ibn Ja'far (AS).

3.13. Tenth Imam (AS)

Imam Ali al-Naqi (AS) was born on the fifteenth of the Month of Dhul Hijj'a or second of Raj'ab in the year 212 AH in Sariya in vicinity of the Holy City of Medina; his father was Imam Muhammad al-Taqi (AS) and his mother was Sam'anah. Imam Muhammad al-Taqi (AS) with God's command appointed his Imam Ali al-Naqi (AS) to Caliphate and Imamate.[1] He was only eight years old when his father left the world; and at the same young age acquired Imamate, but was completely aware of divine knowledge. He was unique and matchless in knowledge and wisdom. His decent conduct, vast knowledge, and piousness of that noble one absorbed and attracted the people towards him.

The Abbasid Caliph Muttawakil was afraid that people would be inclined towards him and would gather around him thus causing a threat to his

---

[1]. *Ithbat al-Huda*, v. 6, p-208; *Irsh'ad* of Shaykh Mufid, p-308.

government; due to this reason he called the Imam (AS) from Medina to Samara in the year 243 AH and kept him under his severe vigilance. Imam Ali Naqi (AS) lived in this world for a period of only forty two years and was continuously under the pressure of Abbasid Caliphs and was martyred on the twenty-seventh day of Jum'ada al-Thani or third of the Month of Raj'ab in the year 254 AH, in Samara and was buried there.

3.14. Eleventh Imam (AS)

The eleventh Imam Hasan al-Askari (AS) was born on the eighth or fourth of the Month of Rabi al-Thani in the year 232 AH in the Holy City of Medina. His father was Imam Muhammad Taqi (AS) and his mother was Hudeth. Imam Muhammad al-Taqi (AS) with God's Command, appointed his son Imam Hasan al-Askari (AS) to Caliphate and Imamate.[1] Imam al-Askari (AS) too like his father was under severe vigilance in the City of Samara and was also in prison for a period of his blessed life. People were not able to see him freely in order to benefit from his knowledge and wisdom. But in spite of that narrations have remained from him as his legacy; his pleasant conduct, virtues and knowledge are not hidden from anyone. Imam Hasan al-Askari (AS) lived in this world for only twenty eight years and was martyred on the eighth day of the Month of Rabi al-Awwal in the year 260 AH and was buried there.

---

[1]. *Ithbat al-Huda*, v.6, p-269; *Irsh'ad* of Shaykh Mufid, p-315.

3.15. Twelfth Imam (AS)

The twelfth Imam of Shi'a, Muhammad ibn al-Hasan (AS) was born in Samara on the fifteenth of Sh'aban in the year of 255 AH; his titles are al-Mahdi, the one who would rise up *(Qa'im)* and Lord of the Age *(Sahib al-Zaman)* and Proof of God *(al-Hujjah)*. His father was Imam Hasan al-Askari (AS) and mother was Narjis. Imam Hasan al-Askari (AS) with God's Command appointed his son Imam Muhammad al-Mahdi (AS) to Caliphate and Imamate. In many of the narrations that have reached us through the Holy Prophet (SAW), he said: ***"The ninth son from the lineage of Imam al-Husain (AS) would have my name and would be the Promised Guide (Mahdi M'aood)."*** The Holy Prophet (SAW) and Infallible Imams (AS) have informed that that the son of Imam Hasan al-Askari (AS) is the Promised al-Mahdi (AS), and he would remain hidden for a prolonged period from our sights. When God would deem it to be expedient, he would appear and would reform the world through expanding justice and equality; he would rule over the entire earth, would make Monotheism and God's worshipping as general and would officially declare the sacred religion of Islam for all of mankind.

In accordance with the forecast of the Holy Prophet (SAW) and information and narrations from the Infallible Imams (AS), God gave a son to Imam Hasan al-Askari (AS) named, Muhammad

(AS); a group of very close companions and a number of people in his inner circle who were trusted by Imam Hasan al-Askari (AS) have seen that child and testified about his presence. The Imam of the Age (AS) at the time of the demise of his father was only five years old and acquired Imamate after him. Since the Abbasid Caliphs had heard about the indications of Imam al-Mahdi (AS) and were learned about the Holy Prophet's (SAW) traditions that the son of Imam Hasan al-Askari (AS) is the promised savior who would confront oppression and injustice and would make the government of tyrants upside down; they had a serious determination that if there is a child from Imam Hasan al-Askari (AS) they would kill him in order to remove the great danger from their path.

It was due to this reason as well as other considerations, the Imam of the Age (AS) was forced to remain hidden from sights and should live secretly, but his link with the people was not completely severed, rather it was possible that through the means of specially appointed people who were called as his deputies *(wakil or nayab)*, people could have communicated with the Imam of the Age (AS) and could have obtained the answer to their requests. His famous deputies are four people as follows:

1. Othman ibn S'aeed

2. Muhammad ibn Othman

3. Husain ibn Rooh

4. Ali ibn Muhammad Samari

These four people were appointed as his
deputies one after another, then his smaller
occultation *(gheebat-e-sughra)* was completed and
official communication with Imam (AS) was
terminated and greater occultation had begun.
Currently Imam (AS) lives in greater occultation
(ghaybat-e-kubra); he moves among the people,
participates in congregations but does not introduce
himself. This condition will continue until the
general circumstances of the world become suitable,
and the ground for the establishment of a single
Islamic Government of the world becomes readied.
And a majority of the people would be inclined
from the profundities of their heart and soul for the
ruling of a system based upon monotheism, and
would consider a solution of their problems only
through obedience of God's Commandments after
becoming completely disappointed from
everywhere, and with severe intensity of their
infliction with tyranny and injustice would be put
out of patience by harassment.

At that time the Lord of the Age, Imam al-
Zaman (AS), will appear and through mighty power
that he would have at his disposal; he would turn
the institution of oppression and injustice upside
down and through the execution of the divine
commandments would fill the world with justice
and equality. We Shi'a during the period of his

occultation have the obligation of waiting for his arrival: We abstract the most subtle programs of social commandments of the Holy Qur'an and introduce them to the attention of mankind; prove distinctions and advantages of divine laws to mankind. We bring attention of mankind towards the divine programs and laws; confront with false ideologies and fallacies; endeavor to provide the required preparations and preliminaries for establishment of Islamic Government for the entire world. Meanwhile through abstracting design and plans of solutions of the world's problems from the Holy Qur'an and narrations, provide them to reformers of mankind; through making the thoughts of human beings enlightened, accordingly prepare ourselves for the Imam's (AS) appearance and the formation of the government of justice and equity.

3.15.1. Our Belief Regarding Imams (AS)

1. The Imams (AS) are completely immaculate from sins, mistakes and blunders.

2. They are thoroughly knowledgeable about all divine commandments and laws; knowledge and information which are required for guidance and spiritual instructions have been provided to them.

3. None of the commandments are introduced by them nor are they its commentators.

4. They practice all religious commandments and believe truthfully in them; they

are decorated with decent, righteous conduct and are the best individuals of humanity and are the complete manifestation of the religion.

5. They are human beings and are servants of Allah, the Most High, just like any other human beings; they are His creatures susceptible to sickness and death; they are not gods and creators of existences.

6. Eleven of them were martyred. The Twelfth Imam (AS) is the immediate son of Imam Hasan al-Askari (AS); he is still alive and his appearance is awaited.

3.16. Shi'a

Those who consider Imam Ali ibn Abu Talib (AS) as immediate caliph and successor of the Holy Prophet (SAW) are called Shi'a. The Imamiyeh Shi'a regard Imam Ali ibn Abu Talib (AS) and his eleven infallible sons as Imam and leaders and obey their sayings and deeds. A true Shi'a is someone who follows Imam Ali (AS) and infallible Imams (AS) and their narrations and deeds as their model. Imam al-Baqir (AS) said to Jabir: *"O Jabir! Is it sufficient for a person only to say this much amount that: 'I am a lover of Ahl al-Bayt (AS)?' By God he is not our Shi'a but that he should be pious and obey God. O Jabir earlier, my Shi'a were identified for these characteristics: Hospitability, being trustworthy, remembering God, prayer, fasting, goodness towards parents, helping neighbors and the destitute, orphans and those who were under debt, righteousness and being reciters of the Holy Qur'an. They did not say a thing about the people except goodness; they were trustworthy of the people.'*

"Jabir replied: 'O son of the Holy Prophet (SAW)! At this time I do not know any one possessing these characteristics.' Imam (AS) replied: 'O Jabir different beliefs should not make you confused and to fall down to commit a mistake. Is it sufficient for the prosperity of a person that he should hold to this much that: I am lover of Imam Ali (AS), but does not do God's commandments? If someone says that: I am lover of the Holy Prophet (SAW) but does not follow his words and deeds, the friendship of the Holy Prophet (SAW) should not become the means of his prosperity while the Holy Prophet (SAW) was superior to Imam Ali (AS). O Shi'ah! Be afraid of God, and obey His commandments. God does not have family ties or relationship with anyone; the most honorable person near God is the person who is the most pious and foremost in performance of deeds. O Jabir! By God, there is no means of God's nearness except obedience to His Commandments. Freedom from hell is not in our hands, whoever is obedient to God is our friend, and whoever rebels against God's Commandments is our enemy. Our vicegerency (vilayat) is not obtained except through the means of righteous deeds and piousness.'"[1]

---

[1]. *W'afi*, v.1, part-3, p-38.

Imam al-Sadiq (AS) said: *"Be pious and righteous; make endeavors in self-purification and cleansing and the performance of virtuous deeds; be truthful, trustworthy, and of pleasant conduct; treat yours neighbors kindly; through the means of your conduct and deeds, invite people towards the true religion. Be a source of our prestige and to keep our head high. With wicked deeds do not provide the means of our shame and degradation. Make your prostrations and genuflections prolonged; because when a slave prolongs his prostrations and genuflections, Satan becomes upset and cries: 'O woe! They have done obedience and I have sinned, they prostrate but I refused to do prostration.'"*[1]

Imam al-Sadiq (AS) said: *"Disciples and helpers of Jesus (AS) were his Shi'a; but his helpers were not better than our Shi'a; because they gave him the promise to help but didn't deliver their promise and did not fight in the path of God. But our Shi'a, since the demise of the Holy Prophet (SAW) until now never refuse from our helping and offered sacrifices for us; were burned in fire, were tortured and severely punished, and were exiled from their homes but did not hold their hands from our help and support."*[2]

---

[1]. *Ibid*, p-61.
[2]. *Safinatul Bih'ar*, v.1, p-73.

3.17. Our Beliefs about Other Muslims

While we have differences of opinion with Sunnis with respect to the issue of caliphate and the succession after the Holy Prophet (SAW), we still regard all Muslims as our fellow brothers; our God is one; our book is the same and our *Qiblah*[1] is the same. We regard their dignity and progress as our own dignity and progress. We account their victory and domination as our own domination and their defeat and degradation is our own defeat and degradation. We are their partners in sharing their happiness and sorrows. In this act we take inspiration from our great leader Imam Ali ibn Abu Talib (AS); if Ali (AS) wanted to defend his legitimate right to take the caliphate he was able to do so, but instead preferred the general interest of Islam and preserving the religion. He not only confronted the caliphs, rather at the sensitive and required moments rushed to their help, and never refused from taking any step in the interest of Islam. We believe that the Islamic world would only remain as a living and powerful nation, could retake its grandeur and majesty, rescue itself from the superimpositions of the aliens, only through taking distance from differences, concentrating its energy toward one objective and all of them should take giant steps in the path of advancement, grandeur and progress of the Islamic world.

---

[1]. The direction of prayer i.e. Holy Mecca [Tr].

Chapter 4: Resurrection or Hereafter

4.1. The Day of Judgment

All divine Prophets and Holy Scriptures are unanimous about this point that the life of a human being does not end at his death. After it another world exists where human beings would see the rewards of their deeds and character. The pious individuals would see a joyful and happy life and would be blessed with dignity and plenty of divine bounties; while the wicked and lewd would have a harsh and painful life and would have a life of torture and punishment. The reality of Judgment and a world after death is a necessity of all heavenly religions, and whoever accepts the Prophets must also accept the Day of Judgment. In order to prove this matter we would describe the following two simple arguments:

First Argument: If you pay attention, proof of the Day of Judgment would become clearly explicated for you:

1. None of the acts are without an aim and objective; whoever does some work also has an objective and goal. The aim and ultimate objective is a thing that motivates the subject to do his work, and in order to accomplish it he makes efforts and endeavors.

2. Although each task is not without an aim and objective, the aims and objectives are not similar; instead they vary with respect to individuals and their tasks. The more a subject is knowledgeable, powerful, and possesses a rational

program; he pursues superior and valuable objectives. A young child who peruses a goal in a childish play would never be equivalent to the goals of an engineer, intellectual and director.

3. The human beings whatever tasks they pursue, desire that through the means of the objective and result of that task, to remove a defect from them in order to achieve more perfection. For example when we eat food it is because of the reason that we feel in ourselves a feeling of hunger, we eat food in order to remove the defect caused by hunger. But for divine acts this context is not valid, because God is not imperfect so that through the means of a result or objective, a task should remove His defect and achieve more perfection. Therefore, it could be said that the result of a task is not applicable to Him but it reaches to his creatures. The objective is not to achieve perfection or to be benefitted rather it is to enrich and to bestow perfection upon His creatures.

Persian Verse:

"Man na kardam khalq ta sudi kunam,
Balkeh ta bar bandgan judi kunam."

English Translation:

I did not create creation to be benefited
Instead it was to bestow mercy upon
my servants."

98

4. God has created human beings with a most superior existence and in the structure of his existence and has utilized thousands of delicacies and sophistications that the intellectuals, no matter how hard they try to comprehend it, they encounter extremely amazing mysteries in a manner that it could be said:

God, the Wise, has made the small-world *(jah'an-e-asghar)* the human being's skeleton as a sample of the greater world's *(jah'an-e-akbar)* existence and has placed a vast universe in his limited body structure. He has created water, earth, air, plants, animals, stars and other existences to meet his requirements; has accumulated thousands of amazing mysteries in the heart of the material world so that the human being could utilize it. Also he has equipped the human existence with amazing intellectual thoughts in order to explore the hidden mysteries of the world of existence, and to utilize the precious treasures of the material world as well as to conquer it. Because of the above mentioned matters, now let us think; could it be said that: The God, the Wise, created amazing and mysterious human existence, and for his utilization commissioned a most outstanding organization of the material world, only for an insignificant period to live in this world and should simply change the vast divine bounties into a different form, then should die and be annihilated? If such is the case then is not the entire creation of God nonsense, null and void? Your faculty of reason would never believe about such an issue and the sacred existence of God is too glorified for such a nonsensical task. Non-existence and annihilation could not be the ultimate goal of creation and ultimate result of the human being's lives, because the accomplishment of a cherished goal requires that the existence should be made more perfect and precious instead of terminating his existence and destroying the book of his age.

Our faculty of reason states that: Since God does not have any need of creation of existences, He does not create them with the intention of earning a profit, and a nonsensical and null and void act is not issued by Him. Therefore, inevitably He has created human beings for the objective of a higher, superior, and precious objective and their lives are not limited to only a transient few days of life of this world and through the arrival of his death, their lives are not ended and the book of their deeds are not closed. Our faculty of reason states that: After this world there should be another world or hereafter; the period of his transient living in this world with so many hardships should only be a preliminary for an eternal life in the hereafter and achieving the prosperity and infinite ease and comfort in the next world. God's intentions were that a human being in this world should make progress and should acquire for him perfections and excellent habits in order to live a prosperous life full joy and heavenly bounties forever in the eternal world.[1]

Second Argument:

Some human beings are pious and righteous; they are well-farers of the people, help their inferiors and fellow human beings, treat orphans with compassion, do favors towards the destitute and distressed, their conduct is good, they do not speak lies, cheat, oppress others, usurp people's belongings; they offer their prayers and fast, practice their mandatory obligations and prevent others from committing sins.

Another group is wicked and indecent, they oppress and do injustice to their fellow human beings, usurp rights of the others, are liars rude, and traitors, do not offer divine mandatory obligations, neither do they offer prayers nor do they fast, they do not feel the least embarrassed from indulging in illegitimate and shameful acts, and like beasts day and night are busy in oppression, transgression, and fulfilling their carnal desires. These two groups continuously had been existing and would remain always, and do not see the punishment of their deeds in this world. We know so many such persons that throughout their lives were engaged in the path

---

[1]. God in the Holy Qur'an has pointed out about the same reason when He says: *"Did you think that We had created you for a playful purpose and that you were not to return to Us?"*

—The Holy Qur'an (23: 115)

of oppression, transgression, usurpation of people's belongings, sinning, and perusing their carnal desires. They left the world in affluence, luxuries, and joyful without seeing the retribution of their evil deeds. On the other side there were many pious and righteous individuals who remained in complete poverty and harsh conditions without seeing rewards of their good deeds.

Therefore, should there not be another world where deeds of the people could be scrutinized, where the righteous ones should obtain excellent rewards for their good deeds and the wicked ones should be punished for their evil deeds? If the age of the people would end in this very world and their book of deeds becomes completely closed and annihilated then in that case would not the creation of human beings be a nonsensical act opposite to the justice and wisdom of God-Almighty? Would your faculty of reason like it, that the righteous and pious individuals would be treated similarly like the wicked and lewd people and their deeds should not be scrutinized? Can such an indecent and inappropriate thing be related to God?[1] If there is no Hereafter and the Day of Judgment of deeds, dispatching of the divine messengers for implementation of divine Command of encouraging good and forbiddance of evil would be

---

[1]. God in the Holy Qur'an has pointed about the same meanings and says: *"Shall We treat those who believe and do good works as those who spread corruption in the earth; or shall We treat the pious as the wicked?"*
                                    —The Holy Qur'an (38:28)

irrational and without any profit; if there exists no accounting of deeds and reward and retribution then why should people obey the commands of God and heavenly messengers?

4.2. Death

Death means separation of the soul from the body; Islam tells us: A human being is not annihilated through the means of death; instead it is transferred to another world and from this life enters into another form of life. The Holy Prophet (SAW) said: *"You have not been created for annihilation instead for eternal life; it is not but your transfer from this world to another world."*[1]

From the Islamic point of view the separation of the soul from the body is not done for all human beings in a similar manner; individuals who are sinners, their inclination is more towards the world are not linked with the hereafter are hopeless, and give up their soul with hardship and difficulty. But the individuals whose deeds are decent and do not have much attachment with this world, instead they have more inclination and attachments towards God and hereafter give their soul comfortably and with ease.[2]

---

[1]. *Bih'ar al-Anw'ar*, v. 6, p-249.
[2]. *Ibid*, p-145.

4.3. Interval between Death and Resurrection

Regarding the basic reality of Resurrection and life after death, our faculty of reason proves it for us however regarding the quality and how it is supposed to be, the reason cannot be our guide; instead we are helpless but to benefit from verses of the Holy Qur'an and sayings of divine messengers and religious saints. It could be understood from the Holy Qur'an, traditions of the Holy Prophet (SAW) and Infallible Imams (AS) that before the Day of Judgment and general resurrection, another world exists where human souls live between death and resurrection called *barzakh* which is a means between the world and hereafter. When a person dies in the beginning he enters into *barzakh*, where he would have some sort of special life. In the beginning of the spiritual life that starts from the grave an overall questioning is conducted in which a person's faith and belief are reviewed; if his beliefs were true and he had righteous deeds, a door from paradise opens and he is assigned on the path of paradise. He utilizes bounties of paradise and remains in waiting for the occurrence of resurrection and to receive eternal heavenly bounties.

If a person happens to be with bad belief and deeds he is assigned to the path of hell and a door from the door of hell opens for him. He would remain in punishment and torture until the occurrence of the resurrection and would suffer a bitter and unpleasant life and have fear of the arrival of the Day of Judgment and severe punishment of hell; he would remain in anxiety and horror.[1]

4.4. Day of Judgment and General Resurrection

The Holy Qur'an and traditions of the Holy Prophet (SAW) and Infallible Imams (AS) describe the Day of Judgment in the following manner: *"The sun and moon would become dark and without illumination, mountains would become scattered,*

---

[1]. God has said in the Holy Qur'an: *"And behind them is a barrier until the day when they are raised."*
—*The Holy Qur'an (23:100)*

"And call not those who are slain in the way of Allah 'dead.' Nay they are living, only ye perceive not.
—*The Holy Qur'an (2:154)*

"Think not of those who are slain in the way of Allah, as dead. Nay, they are living. With their Lord they have provision."
—*The Holy Qur'an (3:169)*

The Holy Prophet (SAW) said that: *"The grave is the prime station of hereafter, whoever is rescued from that later on the task would become easier upon him, and whoever is not rescued from it the later punishments are not easier than it."*
—*Bih'ar al-Anw'ar, v. 6, p-242*

Imam al-Sajjad (AS) said that: *"The grave is either a garden from gardens of the paradise or is a trench from trenches of the hell."*
—*Bih'ar al-Anw'ar, v. 6, pp-214, 202-282*

oceans would become burnt and without water; the solar system would be annihilated; the earth and heaven would be changed into a different form; then all dead would be resurrected alive and would be brought to accounting of their deeds. All accounts of deeds of the people are proven and recorded in a book of deeds; even a tiny act of theirs would neither be forgotten nor removed. On the Day of Judgment curtains would be rolled up from human eyes, they would witness their character and deeds personally; then the accounting of deeds would begin and would be scrutinized with precise accuracy. Unbelievers and sinners who are not pardonable would be sent to hell. The believers and righteous persons would go to paradise.

"The sinners who are illegible for pardon, since they were under punishment in the barzakh and have already tasted the result of their evil deeds; through means intercession of the prophets and infallible Imams would be pardoned, eventually the illumination of monotheism would remove the darkness of their sins and they would enter into paradise. For believers and righteous persons the accounting of deeds would be done easily and they would be sent to the paradise sooner; but with respect to the unbelievers and a majority of sinners, it would be very hard. Even the smallest of their deeds and actions would be severely scrutinized; they would remain stopped in resurrection for a prolonged period and with a great deal of hardship and after passing through

various stages, would end up in their accounting."[1]

4.5. Paradise

Paradise is a place where decent and righteous individuals would be taken; different kinds of blessing, bounties, resources and means of comfort and joy are present there; whatever a human being could imagine and desires is available therein.[2] The bounties of paradise are far superior and better to the bounties of the world, and no one has ever heard or seen them. There is no discomfort and hardship in them; whoever would enter paradise would have eternal life and would remain therein forever. Paradise consists of different ranks and positions and everyone in accordance to his virtues and perfections of self and decent conduct would be assigned an appropriate place accordingly.[3]

4.6. Hell

Hell is the place of unbelievers and wicked ones; every sort of horrible punishment and torture is implemented therein. The individuals who would

---

[1]. *Bih'ar al-Anw'ar,* v.7, pp, 54-237
[2]. **"Therein are brought round for them trays of gold and goblets, and therein is all that souls desires and eyes find sweet. And ye are immortal therein."**
—*The Holy Qur'an (43:71)*

[3]. *Bih'ar al-Anw'ar*, v. 8, pp, 71-322

go to hell would be under punishment with intense hardships and discomfort; the punishments of hell are so severe that it is impossible to describe them. The fire of hell not only burns the body but also the burns souls and hearts of individuals, and it oozes from the fountainhead of its essence and sets the entire existence ablaze.[1] The dwellers of hell consist of two groups: The first group consists of unbelievers, who are completely deprived of the illumination of faith, and God's worshipping; this group would always remain in hell under the intense punishment and torture. The second group consists of God worshippers and faithful who indulged in sinning due to the weakness of their belief and due to this reason deserved the punishment in hell. This group would remain under hell's punishment temporarily, but eventually the illumination of Monotheism would be dominated over the darkness of their sins and either through the direct pardon of God or through intercession of the chosen prophets would be rescued from hell and would enter paradise. Hell consists of different ranks of various sorts of punishment; everyone would be assigned a place in accordance[2] to the degree of his sins and would be punished with special sorts of punishment accordingly.

---

[1]. *"(It is) the fire of Allah kindled.*

—The Holy Qur'an (104:06)

[2]. *Bih'ar al-Anw'ar*, v. 8, pp, 222-374

4.7. Intercession

The issue of intercession has been mentioned in Holy Qur'an and plenty of narrations have been issued by the Holy Prophet (SAW) and Infallible Imams (AS) about it. In a manner that the reality of intercession cannot be denied; in general it could be concluded from narrations that the Holy Prophet (SAW) and Infallible Imams (AS) would act as an intercessor with respect to some of the sinners and say: *"O God! Although this person is a sinner and deserves punishment but because of the means of that particular outstanding virtue and goodness that he has or through Your Own forgiveness and benevolence or through the dignity that we have near You, we request to consider his sins as unseen and delete the crime of his deeds with Your compassion."* Their request of his intercession would be accepted and the relevant person would be blessed with Compassionate God's forgiveness and benevolence. Because of the verses of the Holy Qur'an and narrations, the reality of basic intercession cannot be denied, however some of the points should not be neglected as follows:

1. The intercessors would not offer intercession without permission and command of the God of the Worlds.

2. The place of intercession is at resurrection and after the accounting of deeds. It is here that since the file of deeds is scrutinized its obligation should be explicitly declared, and due to this reason

the intercessor requests for his intercession and sends him to paradise, who was otherwise destined to go to hell because of his sins. But in the *barzakh*, any intercession is not available and the sinning person inevitably must see torture and punishment in accordance with his deeds; although it is possible that there too due to intercession of the Holy Prophet (SAW) and Infallible Imams (AS) he might be given some sort of reduction in his punishment, but this does not constitute as an intercession.

3. The intercessors themselves have said: *"You should try your best to appear in resurrection in the form of a human being so that we could do intercession for you. Therefore, if the beastly sins reach to a point that would metamorphose human essence entirely, thus making his appearance in the form of a wild beast, there is no room for his intercession. Anyhow for intercession merit and worthiness are essential."*

4. Regarding some of the sins the intercessors, like renunciation of prayers, have said: *"Our intercession would not include this group."*

5. Therefore on the basis of the above mentioned matters a human being should not feel proud because of the promise of intercession and do sins; because someone who indulges in sinning with the hope of intercession is like an individual who is poisoned and exposes himself to the danger of hoping that the doctor and medicine would be able to save him.

110

4.8. Repentance

It could be understood from the verses of the Holy Qur'an and narrations of the Infallible Imams (AS) that a sinner, if before his death repents and is ashamed of his evil deeds, his sins are forgiven and wouldn't be scrutinized for his deeds on the Day of Judgment.[1] Therefore, the door of repentance and return remains always open for all sinners and none should be hopeless of God's blessing; but lest we think that whoever simply recites the phrase of: *"O God forgive me (Astaghfirullah)"* and through the pressure of nerves sheds a tear from his eyes, repents and would be blessed with forgiveness; instead, real repentance requires conditions that Imam Ali (AS) has pointed out. Imam Ali (AS) said: *"There are six things necessary for repentance:*

1. He must be really ashamed from the past sins.

2. He must seriously be determined that he would not commit sins in the future.

3. If people owe something upon you; you must pay them all of their dues.

4. The mandatory obligations not offered must be offered as make up *(Qad'a).*

---

[1]. *W'afi*, 1, part-3, p-183

5. The flesh that has been grown upon the body through utilization of illegitimate *(har'am)* food should be melted down completely through means of sorrow and grief about the committed sins.

6. As you have tasted the sweetness of sinning, should also tolerate the bitterness and hardship of worshipping, then you must recite the phrase of forgiveness: O God forgive me *(Astaghfirullah)*.[1]

***

---

[1]. *Nahj al-Bal'aghah* (Printed in Egypt), Part-2, p-253.

Chapter 5: Moral Ethics

5. Moral Ethics

The good and evil characteristics are called moral ethics; good characteristics are the virtues that result in attaining perfection and distinction of self *(nafs)* like: justice, hospitability, trust in God, maturity, positive far-sightedness, well-wishing, truthfulness, trustworthiness, being content with the will of God, thanking God, pleasant conduct, contentment, benevolence, bravery, being enthusiastic towards religion and chastity of the female members of the family, equality, observation of bonds of relationship *(silah-rahm)*, goodness towards parents, pleasant behavior with respect to neighbors, good conduct with respect to the people, controlling of selfish whims, and love of God. It is incumbent upon each Muslim to identify good virtues and moral conduct, and should make serious efforts and endeavors in acquiring them.

The wicked and evil characteristics are the characteristics that cause the loss and decadence of the self like: arrogance, egoism, self-praise, oppression, not trusting in God, impatience, cynicism, malevolence, incorrectness, not being content with God, jealousy, thanklessness, tale-bearing, grudge-holding, wrath, immorality, greed, avarice, miserliness, hypocrisy, duality, treachery, extravagance, cowardice with respect to religion and female members of the family, injustice, cutting of family ties, annoyance of parents, annoyance of neighbors, misconduct with the people, love of position, faultfinding, backbiting, flattering, and prolonged desires. It is incumbent upon each

Muslim to identify evil conduct and should make efforts and endeavors to remove it from his self. In order to be prosperous it is necessary to completely control our selfish whims, we must utilize and practice the Islamic moral ethics commandments; one should cleanse and purify one's self from evil and wicked deeds, and should decorate one's self with righteous conduct and superior virtues. Islamic moral ethics commandments are one of the most important chapters in Islam; it has paid special attention towards moral ethics. The Holy Prophet (SAW) has considered self-struggle as a greater struggle *(jihad-e-akbar)*[1]; he said: ***"I have appointed in order to complete the righteous conduct among the people.***[2] Since all human deeds stem from the characteristics of his self, therefore the first priority should be to endeavor to reform one's self.

---

[1]. *Was'a'il al-Shi'ah*, The Book of Crusade, p-122
[2]. *Muhajj'atul Bayd'a* of Faiz Kashani, v.2, p-312

Chapter 6: Branches of Religion

6.1. Branches of Religion

God-Almighty has determined a series of commandments and practical programs for us that if they are practiced, our lives of the world would be administered in an excellent manner and would be prosperous and would also make us prosperous and righteous in the hereafter. These commandments are called as branches of the religion *(Fru'-e-din)*. There are plenty of branches of religion but the most important among them consist of eight things named as: Prayer, fasting, charity, one fifth annual saving *(khums)*, hajj, jihad, encouraging of good and forbiddance of evil.

6.2. Prayer

The compulsory prayers consist of six types as follows:

1. Daily prayers

2. Prayer of signs

3. Prayer of the dead body

4. Prayer of circumambulation *(tawaf)*

5. Prayers which become compulsory upon an individual due to taking of an oath, promise, or offering a vow (solemnized to God).

6. Compulsory prayers that have not been offered by a father (but has not been done as a disobedience, and he was able to offer them as a make-up) thus are incumbent upon the elder son to offer them as make-up *(qad'a)* prayers.

Daily Prayers

Prayers are pillars of the religion and bring a servant nearer to the God; the Holy Prophet (SAW) said: ***"By God my intercession does not include anyone who considers the prayer insignificant and is negligent towards it. "***[1] It is incumbent upon each Muslim to offer five times prayers daily: in the morning two units, four units at noon, four units in the afternoon, three units in the evening and four units at night.

Time of Prayers

The time of Morning Prayer is from the breaking of the whiteness of dawn until sunrise. The time of the Noon and Afternoon prayer is from noon until sunset coinciding with the religious time of the evening prayer. The time of Evening and Night prayer is from sunset until religious midnight, which is approximately at eleven past fifteen minutes.

---

[1]. *W'afi*, v.2, Part-5, p-13.

6.3. Ablution

Before offering prayer one should perform ablution in the following manner:

1. He should make intentions *(Niyyat)* that he is doing ablution for the pleasure of God.

2. He must wash the face, from top down starting from the forehead where hairs start growing to the chin.

3. He must wash the right hand, from the elbow to the tip of fingers from the top down.

4. He must wash the left hand from the elbow to the tip of fingers from the top down.

5. He must pull the right hand with its own moisture to the front of head from the top down.

6. He must pull the right hand up with its own moisture over the top of the feet from tip of the toes to the leg intersection.

7. He must pull the left hand with its own moisture over the top of the feet from the tip of the toes to the ankles.

6.4. Adhan (Call to Prayer[1])

It is recommended to recite the call of prayer before offering of prayer as follows:

1. God is greater than can be described *(Allahu Akbar)*
Four times.

2. I bear witness that there is no god except God *(Ashhadu 'an l'a 'ilaha 'illallah)*
Two times.

3. I bear witness that Muhammad is the Prophet of God *(Ashhadu anna Muhammadan rasul Allah).*
Two times.

4. Come for prayer *(Hayya 'alassal'ah)*
Two times.

5. Come for salvation *(Hayya 'alal fal'ah)*
Two times.

6. Come for the best deed *(Hayya 'al'a khayril 'amal)*
Two times.

---

[1]. The sources of imitation *(marajeh taqlid)* have written that: The phrase Imam Ali (AS) is the saint of God *(Aliyan waliyull'ah)* is not the part of call and establishment of the prayer *(Adh'an and 'Iq'amah)* but it is recommended that after recital of Muhammad (SAW) is the Prophet of God, it should be recited with the intention of (making) a gift looked upon as bringing blessing or good luck *(tabbaruk), Tawdih al-Mas'a'il* issue #919.

7. God is greater than can be described *(Allahu Akbar)*
Two times.

8. There is no god but God *(L'a 'il'aha illall'ah)*
Two times.

6.5. Call for Establishing of Prayer

It is recommended to recite the call for establishing or readiness of prayer *('Iq'amah)* before offering of prayer as follows:

1. God is greater than can be described *(Allahu Akbar)*
Two times.

2. I bear witness that there is no god except God *(Ashhadu an la 'ilah illallah)*
Two times.

3. I bear witness that Muhammad is the Prophet of God *(Ashhadu anna Muhammadan rasul Allah)*
Two times.

4. Come for prayer *(Hayya 'alassal'ah)*
Two times.

5. Come for salvation *(Hayya 'alal fal'ah)*
Two times.

6. Come for the best deed *(Hayya 'al'a khayril 'amal)*
Two times.

7. Get ready for the prayer *(Qad q'amat as sal'at)*
Two times.

8. God is greater than can be described *(Allahu Akbar)*
Two times.

9. There is no god but God *(La'ilah'a illalla'ah)*
One time.

6.6. Instructions for Recitation of Prayer

In the prayer the followings acts should be performed as follows:

1. Intention *(Niyyat)*: After standing while facing Mecca *(Qiblah)*, do intention, for example offering two units of the Morning Prayer for the pleasure of God.

2. Recitation of Glorification of God by Saying God is Great *(Takbiratul 'ihr'am)*: After making the intention raise the hands to the softness of the ears and say "God is Great" *(Allahu Akbar)*, then one should bring the hands down.

3. Recital: Having recited God is Great *(Allahu Akbar),* start recital of the Surah of Praise *(al-Hamd)* of the Holy Qur'an as follows:

1. In the Name of Allah, the Beneficent, the Merciful.

2. Praise be to Allah, Lord of the Worlds:

3. The Beneficent, the Merciful.

4. Owner of the Day of Judgment.

5. You (alone) we worship; You (alone) do we ask for help.

6. Show us the straight path:

7. The path of those whom You have favored; not (the path) of those who earn Your anger nor of those who go astray.

Bismil-la'hir Rahm'annir-Rahim Alhamdu-lill'ahi rabbil 'a'alamin*Arrahm'ani- rrahim*M'aliki yawmmid-din*Iyy'aka na'abudu w a 'iyy'aka nasta 'in* 'ihdin'a siratal mustaqim*Siratal ladhina 'an'amta 'alayhim ghayril maghdubi 'alayhim waladdallin.

Having recited the Surah of Praise, one of the Surah from the Holy Qur'an is recited e.g. Surah The Purity[1] as follows:

In the Name of Allah, the Beneficent, the Merciful.

1. Say: He is Allah, the One![2]

2. Allah, the eternally besought of all!

3. He does not beget nor was begotten.

4. And there is none comparable unto Him.

Bismil-l'ahir Rahma' nir-Rahim
Qul huwa Allahu 'ahad* Allahus
samad*Lamyalid walam yulad* Walam ya kun
lahu kufu wan ahad.

First Reminder

The Praise and the second Surah in the first and second units *(Rak'ats)* must be recited in all prayers.

---

[1]. Surah The Purity *(al-Ikhlas or al-Tawheed)* takes its name from its subject. It has also been called the essence of the Holy Qur'an. Some authorities ascribe this Surah to the Medina period, and think that it was revealed in answer to a question of some Jewish intellectuals concerning the nature of God. It is generally held to be an early Meccan Surah [Tr].
[2]. The One God, the unique God: Therefore the pronoun He is used and recited for dignity [Tr].

126

Second Reminder

For the men it's incumbent to recite the Surah Praise and other Surah in the Morning and Evening Prayers loudly.

Third Reminder

Raising of the hands at the time of recital of God is Greater than can be described *(Allahu Akbar)* at the time of starting the prayer i.e. saying *Takbiratul 'ihr'am* is only recommended and is not mandatory *(Wajib)*.

4. Bowing *(Ruku')*

Having recited the Surah Praise and another Surah, one should bow *(Ruku')* i.e. bending to the extent that that the hands reach until the knees, then one should recite:

Pure and Glorified is my Lord, the Highest to Whom we offer the Praise.

(Subhan rabbiyal-'azimi wa bihamdihi).

Or should say three times: Glory be to God *(Subhanallahi).*

After completion of bowing *(Ruku')*, one should stand up, take a short pause and it is recommended to recite: God listen to those who offer His praise *(Sami'a All'ahu-liman-hamidah).*

5. Prostration *(Sajdah)*

Having offered the bowing *(Ruku')* we should go to prostration *(Sajdah)* i.e. putting the forehead upon earth or whatever is grown from it - except wearable thing, edibles, and minerals- in a manner that the two palms and knees, forehead and the two large toes of both feet should touch the earth, then we should recite:

Pure and Glorified is the Lord, the Most Supreme to Whom we offer the Praise (Subhan rabbiy al-'al'a wa bihamdihi); or could say three times: Glory be to God *(Subh'anallahi).* After that we should raise our head and sit down a while, and should recite:

I seek forgiveness from my God and toward Him do I turn in repentance *(Astghfirull'aha wa atubu 'ilayhi);* and then go to offer a second prostration and finish it like the first prostration. Then raise our head from the second prostration, sit a while and then stand up for offering the second unit *(raka't)*, and it is recommended that while standing up one should recite:

With the Power of God I stand up and sit *(Bihaw lillahi-wa-quwwati-hi- Aqumu wa 'Aq'udu);* then stand up completely and recite Surah praise and another Surah like the first unit *(Rak'at).*

6. Submission *(Qunut)*

In the second unit *(Rak'at)* having finished recital of the both Surahs, raise both hands in front of the face and recite the following of God's remembrance *(Dhikr)*, e.g. recite:

O God bestow upon us bounties of world and as well as of hereafter and protect us from the punishment of hellfire *(Rabbana 'Atin'a fidduny'a hasnatah wa fil 'Akhirati hasanah wa qin'a 'Adh'a ban-n'ar)*.

Reminder: Recital of Submission *(Qunut)* is not mandatory but has distinction and reward.

7. In the second unit, in all prayers, after the head is raised from the second prostration, one must sit and should recite the testimonies in the following manner:

All the Praise belongs to Allah, I bear witness that there is no god except God Who is One without any partner; and bear witness that Muhammad is His slave and His Prophet; O Allah send greetings upon Muhammad and his holy progeny *(Alhamdulill'ahi 'ashadu an l'a il'ah'a illal l'ahu wahdahu l'a sharika lahu wa ashhadu anna Muhammadan 'abduhu wa rasuluhu; Allahummah salli 'al'a Mumhamd wa 'Ali-Muhammad)*.

8. Salutation *(Salam)*: In the Morning Prayer after recital of the testimonies *(Tashahhud) one* should recite the salutation in the following manner:

Salutation be upon you o prophet and blessings and bounties of God be upon you; salutation upon us and upon pious and righteous slaves; salutations upon you and blessing and bounties of God be upon you, *('Assalamu 'Alayka ayyu han nabiyyu wa rahmatul l'ahi wa baRak'atuhu; 'Assalamu 'alayn'a wa 'al'a 'ib'adill'ahi 'Ass'alihin; 'Assal'amu 'Alaykum wa rahmatull'ahi wa barak'atuhu).* After salutation it's recommended to recite God is Greater than can be described *(Allahu Akbar)* three times while raising hands until the softness of the ears.

Reminder: In the Evening Prayer, after offering the first testimonies *(Tashahhud)* after second unit *(Rak'at)*, one should not offer salutation, but instead should arise. Recite the third unit then sit down and (after the second prostration) recite the testimonies and salutations. Also, in the Noon, Afternoon, and Night Prayers, after recital of the first testimonies in the second unit, one should not offer salutation, instead one should rise, offer the third and fourth units, then sit down after the second prostration and recite the testimonies and salutation.

9. The Four Praises *(Tasbihat-e-arba'ah)*: In the third unit of the Evening prayer and in the third and fourth units of the Noon, Afternoon, and Night

Prayer instead of recitation the Surah Praise and another Surah should recite three times the following:

Glory to God, praise to God, there is no god except God and God is Greater than can be described, *(Subh'ana Allahi wal hamdu lill'ahi wa l'a 'il'aha 'illal l'ahu wallahu akbar)*; or one may recite the Surah of praise one time without the recital of another Surah.

First Reminder

The body of anyone who is offering prayer should be clean; his dress too should be clean and lawful and should not have been prepared with an animal of forbidden meat *(har'am)* or dead.

Second Reminder

In order to offer the prayer one should be clean from having passed gas *(hadath)*, wet-dreams *('ihtil'am)*, in the state of having done sexual intercourse *(janabat)*, monthly period *(hayd)* and bleeding *(nif'as)* at the time of delivery for women.

6.7. Essentials of Prayer

The prayer consists of five essentials as follows:

First: Intention *(Niyyat)*.

Second: Recital of God is Greater than can be described *(Allahu Akbar)*, *Takbiratul* 'ihr'am.

Third: Standing *(Qiy'am)* connected with bowing *(Ruku')* i.e. the standing position from which one goes in to the position of bowing and standing in the state of recital of *Takbiratul-'ihr'am.*

Fourth: Bowing *(Ruku').*

Fifth: Two Prostrations *(Sajdah).*

If anyone of these essentials are more or less, the prayer would be null and void, be it either intentionally or out of negligence.

Invalidities or Cancellation of Prayer

The following acts result in the cancellation of the prayer:

1. The ablution *(Wudu)* being as null and void either intentionally or negligently.

2. Intentionally crying for the world.

3. Intentional laughter.

4. Intentional eating and drinking.

5. Increasing and decreasing one of the essentials either intentionally or negligently.

.

6. Saying Amen *('Amin)* after recital of the Surah Praise *(al-Hamd)*.

7. Offering the prayer with your back towards Mecca *(Qiblah)*.

8. Talking.

9. Indulging in an act that makes the prayer as disorderly.

10. Placing two hands upon each other.

6.8. Prayer of a Traveler

The traveler must recite the four unit prayers as two units of prayers with the following conditions:

1. He should have the intention of travelling at least eight *Farsakh*[1] or going four *Farsakh* and returning four *Farsakh*.

2. He should not be among those who travel very often like a driver or a boat runner whose profession is travelling.

3. He should not be a merchant who does business while travelling.

---

[1]. One *Farsakh* is equal to 6 kilometers [Tr].

4. The journey should not be illegitimate like the journey undertaken for theft and murder, travelling of a wife without her husband's permission or of a son without the permission of his parents.

5. He must not have the intention before travelling eight *Farsakh,* to pass through his homeland, or stay ten days at a place.

First Reminder

The traveler who intends to stay ten days or more at a certain place, so far he/she is there should offer complete prayer. A traveler, who stays at a place for thirty days with uncertainty or contradiction after thirty days must offer complete prayers.

Second Reminder

A person who intends to travel until he has not crossed the border crossing of his/her homeland must not offer broken prayer and should not break his/her fast; as long as the traveler could hear the call of prayer of his/her home city, and could see the walls of his native place he/she has not crossed the border crossing and is not a religious traveler as yet.

6.9. Prayer of Signs

During the period of sun and moon eclipses, occurrences of an earthquake, or an unusual episode that make a majority of the people scared and afraid, it is incumbent upon each Muslim to offer the Prayer of Signs in the following manner:

1. After ablution one should stand towards Mecca *(Qiblah)* and make the intention to recite two units of Prayer of Sign for the pleasure of God.

2. Having made the intention he must raise both hands until the softness of his ears and must say: God is Great *(Allahu Akbar)*.

3. We should recite the Surah of Praise and another Surah and then should go into bowing *(Ruku')* *(bowing down on one's knees during Salat (prayer)* and must offer the remembrance *(Dhikr-e-Ruku')*.

4. We should raise our heads from the bowing *(Ruku')* and should stand, recite the Surah of Praise and another Surah, should bow *(Ruku')* and repeat this procedure in the same manner until recital of five Surahs of Praise, five other Surahs, and five bows *(Ruku's)*.

5. After the fifth bow *(Ruku')* one should go into prostration and should offer prostration like the fortnightly normal prayers.

6. Arise to offer the second unit of Prayer of Signs and perform it like the first unit and after offering the fifth bow *(Ruku')*, one must offer two prostrations.

7. After offering the second prostration one must recite the witnessing and salutations.

Reminder

The period of the Prayer of Signs that are recited for the sun and moon eclipses is from the time of their start until the end, but other prayers whenever they are offered are valid *(ad'a)*.

6.10. Fasting

Fasting is one of the mandatory commandments of Islam; the Holy Prophet (SAW) has said: ***"Fasting is a shield against hell's fire."***[1] God has said: ***"The fast specially belongs to Me and I would bestow its reward."***[2] This worship has uncountable rewards: From the point of view of hygiene is the cause of providing rest to the digestive system of the body and thus helps in soundness of a human being; from the point of view of moral ethics is a sort of practice for piousness and steadfastness with respect to hardships; it reminds the wealthy about hungry and indigents. Imam al-Sadiq (AS) has said: ***"Fasting was***

---

[1]. *W'afi*, v. 2, Part-7, p-5
[2]. *Ibid.*

mandatory so that the wealthy should feel taste of hunger and should think about the hungry, should be kind, and benevolent towards them."[1] It's incumbent on each Muslim to observe fasting during the Holy Month of Ramadan; i.e. from the breaking of the white dawn until evening and they should prevent them from indulging in acts that would make their fast void. The following acts makes fasting void:

1. Eating and drinking.

2. Entering of dirt and thick smoke inside the throat.

3. Throwing up (vomiting).

4. Performance of sexual intercourse.

5. Taking an injection or enema.

6. Submerging the head under the water.

7. Telling a lie about the God and Prophet.

8. Masturbation.

9. Remaining in the state of impurity *(janabat)* due to a wet-dream or sexual intercourse, menstruation or monthly period *(hayd)* and bleeding relevant to childbirth *(nif'as)* for females.

---

[1]. *Ibid.*

Reminder

The above mentioned acts if done intentionally would make the fast void, but if it is done due to negligence and unintentionally, it would not make the fast void; except remaining in the state of impurity in the state any sort of impurity, even it happens due the forgetfulness, would make the fast void.

Those who could break their Fasting

1. The sick person for whom the fasting might be harmful.

2. The traveler with the same conditions that have been described earlier for prayer.

3. A female who sees the blood from monthly period or bleeding relevant to delivery.

Reminder

These three categories must break their fasts and after the removal of the cause they should observe the makeup fast.

4. The pregnant women whose delivery is near and fasting might be harmful either for herself or for the child.

5. The mother who is giving milk to child whose observance of fasting might be harmful for child.

Reminder

For above mentioned two categories after removal of cause, the person should observe makeup fasting and for each fast that they have broken should pay ten *seer*[1] of wheat to the poor.

6. Old men and women for whom observing fasting is difficult.

First Reminder

This group, if they could observe fasting after the Holy Month of Ramadan, they must observe makeup fasts, but if fasting for them is difficult, for them makeup fasting is not required, but for each fast they have missed, they must pay ten *seer* wheat to the poor.

Second Reminder

Whoever does fast breaking without any religious excuse, should observe the makeup for that fast and for every such fast which was not observed, he should observe sixty days of fasting or should feed sixty poor people.

---

[1]. Old unit of weight approximately equal to 75 grams [Tr].

6.11. Charity

Charity is one of the necessary mandatory requirements of Islam. Imam al-Sadiq (AS) has said: *"Whoever does not pay charity is neither a believer nor a Muslim."*[1] Imam Muhammad al-Baqir (AS) has said: *"God has placed charity equivalent with prayer in the Holy Qur'an, hence whoever offers prayer but does not pay charity his prayer too would not be acceptable."*[2] Imam al-Rida (AS) has said: *"Had people paid their charity of their wealth, no one would have been needy."*[3] The payment of charity is mandatory upon: Wheat, Barely, Dates, Raisins, Cows, Sheep, Camels, Gold and Silver. Islam has determined an amount for each of these items that if it reaches to that amount, charity is mandatory otherwise it is not.

The amount required for Wheat, Barley and Raisins

The amount for these four items is 288 *man*[4] of Tabriz and if it is less, it does not require charity. At the time of payment of charity whatever expenses were incurred for forming including the cost of seeds should be subtracted from the product, and one should pay charity for remaining amount.

---

[1]. *W'afi*, v.2, Part-6, p-5.
[2]. *Ibid.*
[3]. *Ibid*, p-6.
[4]. It is a local unit of weight one *man* consists of 40 *seer*; while one *seer* is equal to 75 grams.

Amount of Charity

If farming was done through the means of rain water, river, and aqueduct, one-tenth of it should be paid as charity; if it's irrigated through the means of a well, motor, and bucket, one-twentieth of it should be paid as charity.

The Number or Quantity *(Nis'ab)* liable for Charity Tax for Sheep:

1. Forty sheep
One Sheep.

2. One hundred and twenty one Sheep
Two Sheep.

3. Two hundred and one Sheep
Three Sheep.

4. Three hundred and one Sheep
Four Sheep.

5. Four hundred and above, should be counted into one hundred and then one Sheep for every one hundred should be given as charity.

Reminder

Whoever is the owner of Sheep for eleven months should pay charity in the twelfth month; Charity upon Sheep is only mandatory with the condition that it should graze throughout the year or some period outside in the plains. If it feeds upon fodder cultivated with farming or clipped fodder, charity is not required.

The Number or Quantity *(Nis'ab)* liable for Charity Tax for Cows

Cows have two numbers:

First: Thirty Cows: The charity is one calf that should been entered in the second year.

Second: Forty Cows: The charity is one female calf that should have entered in the third year.

If the number exceeds forty cows, one must adopt the best of the above two criteria. It should be counted in thirties or forties or through both criteria, e.g. sixty Cows should be accounted as two sets of thirties; and seventy Cows should be accounted as one set of thirty and another set of forty.

Reminder

It is mandatory that the cow for charity should not work throughout the year and should graze only fodder in the open pasture (not on collected feed).

The Number or Quantity *(Nis'ab)* liable for Charity for Gold

There are two numbers for Gold:

1. Twenty Religious *Mithqal*[1] (18 *Nakhud* - Pea, 1/5 of a gram): When the gold reaches this much quantity, one-fortieth of it should be given as a charity.

2. When four Religious *Mithqal* is added to the above number; one-fortieth of total quantity should be paid as charity, but if the additional quantity is less than four *Mithqal*, charity should be paid in accordance with first criteria and charity is not incumbent upon additional quantity. After that whatever is added, if it reaches to four *Mithqal* charity should be paid for the total quantity; if less than four *Mithqal* is added charity should be paid in accordance with first criteria but the added quantity does not required charity.

The Number or Quantity *(Nass'ab)* liable for Charity Tax for Silver

There are two numbers for Silver:

1. One hundred and five *Mithqal*, twenty four peas; if Silver reaches to that amount one-fortieth of it should be paid as charity, and if it is less than that quantity, charity is not required.

2. If it is more than 105 *Mithqal* and the additional quantity reaches to 21 *Mithqal*, charity should be given for entire quantity, if it does not

---

[1]. Unit of weight equal to about five grams [Tr].

143

reach this quantity; charity is not required for additional quantity. Only charity should be paid for 105 *Mithqal* and whatever it increases if it reaches to 21 *Mithqal,* charity should be paid for entire additional quantity and it is less than charity should be paid in accordance with earlier requirement and in additional quantity charity is not required.

First Reminder

The charity upon Gold and silver is required only in condition when they are in the form of official currency and should remain in possession of owner for eleventh months.

Second Reminder

The Gold and Silver, until it has not been exited from the required amount for charity; it should be paid for every year, even though charity has been paid for previous year.

Third Reminder

Apparently the aim of Islam is that Gold and Silver currency should not be hoarded and kept in a safe, instead it should be used for economic progress and especially for production.

Utilization of Charity

Charity should be used for the following expanses:

1. Poor *(Faqir)*: i.e. someone who does not have the annual expanses for himself and his family.

2. Destitute *(Miskin)*: i.e. someone whose financial condition is worse than the poor.

3. Welfare Affairs that are beneficial to the general public: Like a mosque, school, bath, bridge, hospital, nursing home, dispensary, and roadways.

4. Someone who is struck in journey without money; he should be given as much to enable him to reach to his hometown.

5. A bankrupt person who is not in a position to pay his debt.

6. In the way of freeing slaves.

7. To an unbeliever about whom it is possible that through means of showing favors towards him, he might be inclined towards acceptance of Islam.

8. To someone who is assigned to collect charity by religious ruler.

Reminder

Had people paid their due charities, it would have been possible for the religious ruler to confront poverty and unemployment and he could have seriously made efforts and endeavors in the affairs of civil development, habitation of cities and village and establishment of welfare organizations.

6.12. One-Fifth Savings of Yearly Income

One of the obligations of Muslims and financial rights of Islam is payment of one-fifth annual savings *(khums)*. In seven instances it is incumbent upon a Muslim to pay one-fifth of his wealth as *khums* as follows:

1. Business Profit: Whoever through means of path of trading, agriculture, industry, worker, employee, and engaged in any other profitable profession earning a profit; whatever he spends in a year for food, clothing, house belongings, purchasing a home, marriage, invitation of guests, and travel does not require *khums*. However after his total annul expenditure, if some amount is still left its mandatory upon him to pay its one-fifth as *khums*.

2. Utilization from a Mine: Like gold, silver, oil, iron, copper, lead, salt, copper, sulfur, and alike.

3. Finding a Treasure

4. Spoils of War

5. Pearls: Those are obtained through the means of taking a dive into the ocean.

6. If a Jew or Christian purchase: A land from a Muslim should pay one-fifth of it or its price as *khums*.

7. Wealth mixed with illegitimate wealth *(har'am)*: The wealth that is mixed with illegitimate wealth, if quantity of illegitimate wealth is not known and does not know its owner, one should pay one-fifth of entire wealth as *khums* so that the remaining becomes legitimate *(hal'al)*.

First Reminder

Upon whoever *khums* is due he should pay it to a just jurisprudent, religious ruler, or his representative, so that it could be utilized in the path of propagation and grandeur of Islam as well as to take care of the Holy Prophet's (SAW) poor decedents *(S'ad'at)*.

Second Reminder

Charity and *khums* are two very heavy amounts for the Islamic budget, which is a very significant amount; if its received accurately and reaches in the hands of a just, religious ruler enabling him to manage the social security affairs of the Muslims, he could combat with poverty, joblessness, and illiteracy, pay attention towards destitute, helpless and poor, and establish welfare organizations beneficial to the general masses in accordance to their needs such as: Hospitals, schools, mosque, baths, roads and bridges etc.

6.13. Hajj

Every Muslim who possesses required physical and financial strength, it is incumbent upon him one time in his life to perform pilgrimage of the Holly Mecca to participate in great and magnificent congregation of Islamic nations. Imam al-Sadiq (AS) said: ***"Whoever dies without undertaking mandatory Hajj-pilgrimage without any religious excuse does not die as a Muslim; he instead would be associated in the ranks of Jews and Christians."***[1] Hajj is one of the greatest worships of Islam and consists of profound and important benefits: A Muslim through means of undertaking a Hajj pilgrimage may strengthen his power of faith and could be connected with the origin of creation. He could learn a lesson of God-worshipping, humility, brotherhood, equality and self-forgiveness in that supreme class of Islamic nourishment.

Muslims from various countries participate in an international congregation thus becoming familiar with habits and traditions of each other; they should learn about the situations of Islamic countries, should become knowledgeable about difficulties and serious dangers facing the Islamic world; should enquire about social, economic, and cultural programs of each other; should discuss

---

[1]. *W'afi*, v. 2, Part-8, p-48.

common interests of the Islamic world; a spirit of solidarity, intimacy, and friendship among them should be strengthened.

Reminder

Hajj is incumbent upon someone who should have financial strength, i.e. if he has taken amount required for expanses of his Hajj-pilgrimage, after his return he should not become helpless and distressed and should be able to continue earning his living through his trade or profession like before.

6.14. Encouraging of Good and Forbidding of Evil

One of the important mandatory commandments of Islam is encouraging of good. It is incumbent upon each Muslim to endeavor in the path of propagation of Islam and its commandments; one should make people well familiar with religious obligations and good deeds. If he saw someone who is not doing his obligation he should persuade him to do his obligation. This is known as encouraging of good *(amr bil m'aruf)*. Forbidding of evil *(Nahy 'an al-Munkar)* and is also one of the great mandatory commandments of Islam. It is incumbent upon each Muslim to confront corruption and oppression; he should prevent others from evil and illegitimate acts; if he sees someone acting against the commandments and instructions of God he should warn him about the evil of that task and to the extent possible, he should do it seriously; he should stood against that task; this act is called as forbiddance of evil *(nahy 'an al-Munkar)*.

Encouraging of good and forbidding of evil is one of the greatest obligations of Islam. If this obligation is practiced the laws and commandments of religion would remain forever and would be executed. Islam expects all Muslims as personally responsible for the execution of religious commandments; it is mandatory upon all Muslims to be vigilant of each other. It is incumbent of Muslims to defend their religious commands and they should make efforts and endeavors for their preservation and implementation. Every Muslim is obliged that he himself should perform good deeds, should persuade others to do good deeds; he should prevent himself from the performance of evil and illegitimate acts as well and should prevent others in indulging in divine forbidden acts. The relevant program is one of the grandeur of Islam and is accounted as one of special programs of the Holy Qur'an. It considers undertaking this heavy responsibility as a code of superiority of the Muslims. God said in the Holy Qur'an:

"Ye enjoin right conduct and forbid indecency; and ye believe in Allah."

—The Holy Qur'an (3:110)

Again He said:

"And let there be from you a nation who invite to goodness, and enjoin right conduct and forbid indecency."

—The Holy Qur'an (3:104)

Imam al-Rida (AS) said: *"Engage in encouraging of good and forbidding of evil. If you do not practice this obligation then wicked people would dominate you, then whenever your righteous pray and cry due to oppression and tyranny their prayers shall not be accepted."*[1] The Holy Prophet (SAW) said: *"So far as my community continues to encourage good and forbid evil and cooperate in this task, the status of their congregation would remain good and respectable, but when they would give up this obligation, blessings would be taken away from them, some of them would be dominated upon others and they would not find a redresser of their grievances upon the earth and heaven."*[2]

Imam Ali ibn abu Talib (AS) said to his companions: *"If you are encountered with danger and hardship, let your wealth be sacrificed for yourselves, and if danger threatens your religion then sacrifice yourselves in support of your religion; know that the unfortunate is the one who let his religion go away from his hands, and the*

---

[1]. *Was'a'il al-Shi'ah*, v. 11, p-349.
[2]. *Ibid*, p-398.

robbed one is a person who has allowed his religion to be stolen.[1]

The encouraging of good and forbidding of evil *(amr bil ma'ruf wa nahy 'an al-Munkar)* is done in the following stages:

First Stage

First with polite manner gently, the goodness and evilness of a deed should be proven for a person and with admonishment and guidance he should be induced to undertake good deeds and to quit evil deeds.

Second Stage

If softness, politeness, guidance, and admonishment did not produce any fruitful result one must do the obligation of encouraging goodness and forbidding evil in a stern manner.

Third Stage

If sternness and a strict tone also did not produce any fruitful result, if he has the power to execute the obligation of encouraging goodness and forbidding of evil with every ways and means, whatsoever that he may have at his disposal, he should prevent that evil act.

---

[1]. *Was'a'il al-Shi'ah*, v. 11, p-451.

Fourth Stage

If after the practicing of admonishment and guidance and sternness and anger, prevention of evil is still not possible for him, then his religious enthusiasm should appear upon his face with signs of severe disapproval and anger so that the person committing that evil deed should realize that he has become an object of isolation, resentment and anger in the sight of people because of his committing that evil deed.

6.15. Some of the Illegitimate Transactions

1. Buying and selling of filth itself like: Urine, excreta, blood and dead things.

2. Buying and selling usurped wealth.

3. Buying and selling resources and particular equipment for illegitimate deeds, like: Gambling equipment, and resources of music and debauchery.

4. Transactions containing interest.

5. Buying and selling alcoholic beverages, liquor, wine, beer, and other items that make a person drunk.

6. Buying and selling things that from the point of Islam are not considered as wealth like: Wild beasts.

7. Selling imitated items; i.e. it essence would have been mixed with other things, like Sheep oil that might have been mixed with cotton or vegetable oils and the buyer is ignorant of it.

8. Selling grapes, raisins, dates, and the like to someone who uses them to make liquor.

6.16. Unclean things

Islam considers few things as unclean *(najis)* and orders the Muslims to stay away from them:

1, 2. Urine and excreta of animals classified of forbidden flesh *(har'am)* that at the moment of their beheading have jumping blood.

3. Semen of animals that have jumping blood.

4. Carcass of an animal that has jumping blood.

5. Blood of animals that have jumping blood.

6. Dogs other than those living in an ocean.

7. Pigs other than those living in an ocean.

8. Unbelievers, i.e. someone who does not believe in the Prophet and God.

9. Alcohols and liquors.

10. Beer.

6.17. Some of the Purifiers

1. Water, everything that is polluted or filthy could be purified through the means of water.

2. Earth, if it is pure and dried could clean the sole of a shoe, its elevated heal, the bottom of cane or stick, automobile wheels, carts, and bicycles, with the condition that through means of walking, the actual filth should be removed.

3. The sun cleans earth, buildings, walls, doors, windows, trees, and similar things with the condition that the actual filth should be removed and its moisture should be dried through means of the sun's rays upon it.

4. Removal of actual filth, when actual filth is removed from an animal's body, it becomes clean and washing with water is not required.

5. Transformation *('istih'alah)*, if an unclean item transforms completely and should turn in the form of a pure thing, like if unclean wood burns and transforms into ashes or the dog into salt marsh or a mine transform into salt.

6.18. Compulsory Washing or Bath

The compulsory washing consists of:

1. Bath of impurity *(janabat)*, bath for monthly period *(hayd)*, bath for bleeding relevant to child birth *(nif'as)*, bath for excessive menstruation *(istih'adah)*, bath for dead body *(mayyit)*, and bath for touching of dead body *(mas-e-mayyit)*. Impurity *(janabat)* could happen in two ways: First sexual intercourse, and second discharge of semen *(mani)*.

Instruction of the Bath *(Ghusl)*

There are few acts mandatory for bath:

1. Intention, bath should be taken for God and one should know which bath he is going to take.

2. After making intention, one should wash the entire head and neck in a manner that not a single spot should remain dry.

3. After washing head and neck all of the right part of body should be washed completely.

4. After washing the right side of body thoroughly, the entire left body part must be washed completely in a manner that no spots should remain dry.

First Reminder

Upon an unclean *(junub)* person, a few things are forbidden *(har'am)*:

156

1. Any part of his body should not touch the writing of the Holy Qur'an, or the Name of God, and the name of Prophets and Imams.

2. Stoppage in mosques and tombs of the Imams.

3. Placing anything in mosque.

4. Reciting Surahs of Prostration.

5. Entrance into the Great Holy Mosque of Mecca *(Masjid al-Har'am)*.

Second Reminder

An unclean *(junub)* person should take a bath for offering prayer and fasting and also a woman who has seen the blood of menstruation *(hayd)* or bleeding relevant to child birth *(nif'as)* must take bath before offering prayer and fasting.

6.19. Instructions for Ablution with Earth or Sand

In ablution with earth or sand *(tayammum)* five things are required:

1. Intention.

2. The palms of the two hands should be put upon the dirt.

3. One must wipe the palms of both hands all over forehead and its both sides from the point where the hairs of head start growing until the eye brows.

4. After that, the palm of the left hand should wipe the back of the right hand starting from wrist until end of finger tips.

5. After that, the palm of the right hand should wipe the back of the left hand starting from wrist until end of finger tips.

First Reminder

Where the use of water is harmful for a person, or one does not have access to water, or the timing of prayer is nearing, one must do *tayammum* for offering of prayer.

Second Reminder

Upon dirt, pebbles, stones, and lumps of earth *tayammum* is permissible.

Third Reminder

If one does *tayammum* instead of a bath, after wiping the forehead, once more the hands should be put upon the dirt and should wipe over the hands.[1]

---

[1]. Readers can consult the instructional journal *(ris'alah 'amaliyah)* of their respective religious authorities *(mar'aji')*.

6.20. Some of the Illegitimate Deeds

Oppression, lying, backbiting, usurpation of people's wealth, faultfinding, gambling, usury, paying of usury, acting as a witness for taking usury, writing of usury receipts, adultery, sodomy, accusing someone for adultery, imitation in quality, hiding of testimony, false testimony, a breach of promise, escaping from the battlefield, drinking alcohol, eating the flesh of a pig, eating of dead things, eating sheep's testicles, eating blood, eating impure things, propagation of corruption and lewd deeds, murder, annoyance of parents, perjury, dishonesty in selling through using smaller weights, helping a tyrant, treachery, misguidance of people, innovations in religion, insulting of a Muslim, hopelessness from God's blessing, cursing, arrogance, taunting, hypocrisy, deceit, misbehavior with neighbors, harming people, bribery, masturbation, stealing, issuance of judgment against God's commandments, decoration of men with gold like wearing a golden ring, or a golden chains for a wristwatch, utilization of gold and silver potteries, and...

6.21. Some of the Compulsions

Prayer, fasting, encouraging of good and forbidding of evil, charity, paying one-fifth from annual savings *(khums)*, Hajj, helping an oppressed, offering witness, defense of the religion, self-dignity, reply to salutations, replying of a letter, obedience of parents, learning of religious commandments, keeping in touch with relatives and kith of kin, to keep one's promise, and being committed towards one's vow (solemnized to God).

6.22. Imitation or Following

God has revealed all commandments and laws which were required for our prosperity in this world and hereafter to the Holy Prophet (SAW) through means of revelation. The Holy Prophet (SAW) too has announced them to people and especially has left them as a trust near the infallible Imams (AS). The successors of the Holy Prophet (SAW) also to the extent it was possible for them made their best efforts and endeavors in the explanation and extension of commandments and have announced for people which have been preserved in the form of narrations and traditions in the books of narrations.

In this period since it is not possible to access Imam al-Mahdi (AS) so that commandments and obligation could be taken from him directly, inevitably we are helpless but to resort to the narrations of the Holy Prophet (SAW) and Ahl al-Bayt (AS) and should take our obligations and duties from them. But understanding narrations and verses of the Holy Qur'an and to diagnose true narrations from a false narration and summation between narrations is a very tedious and a difficult job that everyone is not competent enough to assume such a heavy responsibility. However there are individuals who have expertise in this task, as a result of their suffering hardships in this path for prolonged years, and have learned lessons in different disciplines, which are required for the determination of commandments. They seriously engaged them day and night to such an extent in learning sciences; reviewed existing information and narrations with precise accuracy to achieve the specialty of determining divine commandments and laws. Such individuals are called as jurisprudents and scholars.

We should resort to the jurisprudent in order to determine our own obligations since they are experts and have expertise in this field and in general, intellectuals and wise people always consult relevant specialists in every task and besides, the infallible Imams (AS) themselves have recommended for us to resort to jurisprudents. Of course in order to follow a religious leader *(taqlid)* we should select a jurisprudent that should be more superior, qualified, just, and pious with respect to others and then should act in accordance with his instructions. Jurisprudents in majority of issues have similar beliefs and do not have any differences; but in some secondary issues they have differences of opinion and issues, religious decrees which differ with others.

Here it would be necessary to warn about this matter that God with respect to each issue does not have more than one single command and the real command of God with differences of decrees does not change. The jurisprudent too does not say that God's opinion follows their individual opinions and with differences of their decrees God's opinion also changes accordingly. Here it should be asked why differences in religious decrees started and why do jurisprudents have differences of opinions in some of issues? The answer to this question is: The reason for the differences in religious decrees *(fatwas)* could be from one of the following dimensions.

First: Occasionally one of the jurisprudents in his researching and understanding of God's real command has doubts and was unable to issue a definite decision; due to this reason he has taken the side of precaution in order to preserve God's command and the real matter should not be lost.

Second: Occasionally differences occur from this reason that in the understanding of a narration, which is basis of issuance of religious decree, there are differences of opinions. One says that: Imam (AS) in this narration says like this, while the other says: The aim of Imam (AS) is something else; due to this reason each one issues a decree in accordance of his own understanding.

Third: In some of the issues there exist several narrations in a book of traditions that have contradiction between them, of course a jurisprudent must prefer one of them over the other and should issue his decree accordingly.

Here it is possible that the point of view of jurisprudents may be different. One says: Because of this and that reason he prefers this tradition over the other while other says: Because of this and that reason this tradition has preference over that tradition and each one issues decree in accordance with his own understanding. Of course these secondary differences do not do any damage and among all experts and specialists in different fields these thing exists and are not unusual; you would not find two engineers who do not have any differences of opinion with respect to a certain technical problem. Therefore with the above mentioned discussion it could be concluded:

1. To imitate *(taqlid)* is not a strange and new thing, instead everyone who is helpless, that is to say in affairs that he himself is not specialized, should consult the experts of that field, like in construction affairs we consult an engineer and in case of sickness consult a physician, and about price of commodities we seek consultation of those who are experts in that area. Regarding obtaining God's commandments one must resort to the religious-authority *(mar'aji'-e-taqlid)*, who are specialist of this field.

2. The religious authorities do not issue decrees in accordance with the desires of their hearts and selfish whims instead their criteria in all such issues are the verses of the Holy Qur'an and the narration that has been left by the Holy Prophet (SAW) and the Ahl al-Bayt (AS).

3. The jurisprudents regarding overall Islamic commandments are unanimous and in the majority of cases, even in secondary issues, are unanimous and do not have any differences of opinion.

4. In some of the minor secondary issues that differences opinion among them are seen, they are not in the sense that they like to create differences, instead all of them endeavor to find out God's real commandments which are not more than one and should present it to their followers; but from the point of view of in its determination and their understanding of the issue, regarding real commandment, they have differences of opinion. And in that case they are powerless except to write whatever they have understood regarding that issue. Nevertheless the real commandment is not more than one and followers also do not have any other option except to follow the opinion of their religious authority *("alim)* and therefore possess an excuse before God.

5. Since among all scholars and specialists of different disciplines difference of opinion exists, still people do not pay so much attention towards it and consider it as a normal thing and it has not caused any harm in their social affairs. The difference of opinion among jurisprudents in some of the minor and secondary issues is similar to the other fields and it should not be considered something unusual.

6. Therefore, one should follow a jurisprudent who is more qualified than all other jurisprudents, who is an expert in determining God's commandments; the religious authority must be just, pious, he should act upon his obligations, and should endeavor in the preservation and guarding of religious laws.

Bibliography

1. Ithbat al-Huda, Muhammad ibn Hasan Hur al-'Amily
2. Irsh'ad, Shaykh Mufid
3. Bih'ar al-Anw'ar, Muhammad Baqir ibn Muhammad Taqi Majlisi
4. Al-bid'ayah wa Al-nih'ayah, Abu al-Fida Isma'il ibn Omar Damishqi
5. Tawdih al-Masa'a'il, Religious Authorities
6. Haya't al-Qulub, Muhammad Baqir ibn Muhammad Taqi Majlisi
7. Safinah al-Biha'r, Shaykh 'Abbas Qummi
8. Kashf al-Ghummah, Ali ibn 'Isa Arbili
9. Mahajjah al-Bayd'a, Mulla Mohsen Faiz Kashani
10. Man'aqib A'le Muhammad, Ibn Shahr 'Ashub
11. Nahjul-Balagha, Sayyid Radi
12. W'afi, Mulla Mohsen Faiz Kashani
13. Wasa'il al-Shi'ah Muhammad ibn Hasan al-Hur al-'Amily
14. Yan'a bi' al-Mawwadah, Sulayman ibn Ibrahim Qanduzi

Glossary

1. (SAW): Sallallahu 'Alayhi wa 'Alihi wa Sallam.
   O Allah send salutations upon Muhammad and his family.

2. (AS): 'Alayhi al-Salam.
   Salutations be upon him.

3. (SA): Salamulla'hi 'Alayha.
   Salutations be upon her.

4. (RA): Rizw'anull'ahi 'Alayhi.
   May Allah be pleased with him.

5. (AF): 'Ajjala Allahu Farajahu.
   May Allay quicken his appearance.